William O. Fox

W9-ACA-863

PROPHETIC RELIGION

PROPHETIC RELIGION

By J. PHILIP HYATT

ABINGDON PRESS
New York • Nashville

PROPHETIC RELIGION

Copyright MCMXLVII by Stone & Pierce

All rights in this book are reserved.
No part of the book may be reproduced in any
manner whatsoever without written permission of
the publishers except brief quotations embodied in
critical articles or reviews. For information address
Abingdon Press, Nashville, Tennessee.

Library of Congress Catalog Card Number: 47-2047

SET UP, PRINTED, AND BOUND BY THE
PARTHENON   PRESS,   AT   NASHVILLE,
TENNESSEE, UNITED STATES OF AMERICA

To

The Memory of My Father

ROBERT LEE HYATT

1870 - 1938
A Christian layman who believed
deeply and lived courageously

PREFACE

THIS ATTEMPT TO DISCOVER THE BASIC CHARACTERISTICS OF PROPHETIC religion uses as criterion the work of seven great prophets of the Old Testament, with frequent reference to the prophetic features of the personality and career of Jesus, who in the truest sense was the fulfillment of Old Testament prophecy. It is not a detailed and complete study of the seven prophets, nor does it give a complete history of prophetic religion. Rather, it treats the chosen prophets, who most people will agree are the greatest of the Old Testament prophetic writers, as normative for the type of religious thought generally termed "prophetic."

Today many people talk much *about* the Bible without attending carefully to its actual words. Believing it important that we listen to the prophets as they speak for themselves, I have included in this study numerous quotations from their messages—quotations translated with great care from the original Hebrew and Greek. All these are my own renderings, but I have taken no pains to avoid duplicating words and phrases found in the familiar versions. While it is difficult to transfer Hebrew poetry into adequate English, one should be reminded that the prophets were men of high literary talent. So in translation I have retained the poetic form and have also attempted to convey some of the richness and vividness of the original language.

The Masoretic text of the Old Testament as printed in Kittel's *Biblia Hebraica,* third edition, is usually employed. In a few instances I have translated an emended text, following one of the ancient versions or conjecture. These instances have not, however, been recorded in footnotes. Such notes have been kept to a minimum, since this book is not designed primarily for scholars. Those who know Hebrew will in most cases readily recognize the emendations; those who do not would find the explanatory notes meaningless.

7

Readers will forgive me, I trust, for what may appear to be two oversights in the following treatment.

For one thing, I have touched very little on the psychology of the prophets. This omission is due in part to the fact that our sources are too meager to provide sound basis for such a study, but it stems more from the belief that this approach to understanding the prophets is of little value. They must be evaluated, I believe, by theological rather than by psychological standards. Our generation has too often made the facile assumption that anything can be explained and evaluated in terms of its origin—psychological, historical, or otherwise. We should consider a study of psychological origins—or any other—as only the first halting step on the way to understanding and appreciation, especially in religious matters. It is true that God has sometimes spoken to men more clearly through the psychologically abnormal than through the normal, yet how precarious it would be to conclude that the abnormal is always a revelation of God and the normal never is!

Any extended discussion of the relevance of the prophets and their religion for our own day I have also omitted, only incidentally touching on this topic. Yet I am sure that the prophets do have a profound and far-reaching message for our time, and that we should use all our resources of devotion, research, and insight to apply prophetic principles to our problems today.

This book is addressed to all who have intellectual curiosity about their religion. While it is not written primarily for biblical scholars, I trust they will not find here too much with which to quarrel. I hope that some ministers may be inspired by these chapters to make their own ministry more prophetic, and that some laymen may be encouraged to allow their ministers to be prophets.

It is a pleasure to acknowledge the aid of several friends in the writing of this book. The manuscript was read by Dean John Keith Benton of Vanderbilt University School of Religion; Dean Fleming James of the School of Theology, University of the South; and Professor Millar Burrows of Yale University Divinity School. Professor

PREFACE 9

Edward T. Ramsdell of Vanderbilt University School of Religion read two chapters. I am grateful for the helpful criticism of these friends, but they do not, of course, bear responsibility for the views expressed. To my wife, Elizabeth Bard Hyatt, I am indebted both for constant encouragement and for aid in the preparation of the typescript. Rev. Everett Tilson, Carré Fellow in Vanderbilt University, has kindly aided in the reading of proofs.

J. Philip Hyatt

CONTENTS

11

Chapter I

THE PROPHETS BEFORE AMOS

THE TERM "PROPHETIC RELIGION" IS FREQUENTLY USED IN MODERN religious literature and preaching. It seems generally to refer to that type of religion which emphasizes ethics and the ethical nature of God. A contrast is often expressed or implied with priestly religion and popular religion.

In seeking to define this term more precisely we must study the important characteristics of the religion of the great Old Testament prophets of the period beginning in the middle of the eighth century and ending in the latter part of the sixth century B.C. The term was obviously derived from the words of these men, and we are justified in using their thinking as a criterion for it. These prophets are, in chronological order, Amos, Hosea, Isaiah, Micah, Jeremiah, Ezekiel, and the Second Isaiah. They are the truly major prophets of the Old Testament, regardless of the size of their books.

Although these men furnish the criteria by which to judge prophetic religion, one should not think that they are the only prophets whom God has sent to mankind. Many religions and many ages have produced prophets, or at least men with one or more outstanding prophetic characteristics. There have been true prophets in the history of the Christian church. Indeed, it would be interesting and profitable to trace the stream by which prophetic ideals have been carried through history.

It should not be forgotten that Jesus of Nazareth was in a very true sense a prophet, standing in the tradition established by the major Old Testament prophets. To say this is not to suggest that he was no more than a prophet. To the Christian he is Saviour, Redeemer, Lord. And yet he is far more. None of our conventional categories are adequate to describe him; he broke through all categories, and he gives new meanings to them. Nevertheless, Jesus was known to many people of his own generation as a prophet, and he put a certain stamp of approval upon that designation. At the time of Peter's confession, the disciples told him that some men said he was Elijah or Jeremiah or one of the other prophets (Matt. 16:14). At the time of the triumphal entry into Jerusalem, the multitudes cried out, according to Matthew's version: "This is the prophet Jesus, from Nazareth of Galilee!" (21:11). In fact, Jesus referred to himself indirectly as a prophet when he said, possibly quoting a popular proverb, "No prophet is acceptable in his own country" (Luke 4:24). Luke quotes Jesus as giving this reason for leaving Galilee to make the final journey to Jerusalem: "I must go on my way today and tomorrow and the day following, for it is not fitting that a prophet perish outside of Jerusalem" (13:33).

A noted Jewish scholar, C. G. Montefiore, has rightly pointed out that it was a great achievement to be a prophet of the eighth-century-B.C. type in the first century A.D.[1] The reason is that so much in Judaism crystallized between the eighth century and the first, especially the Law and the canon of Scripture. Jesus, therefore, had much more against which to struggle than did many of the Old Testament prophets.

In our study, then, we shall frequently note how Jesus of Nazareth fits into the pattern of prophet and how he was true to prophetic religion as understood by the great Hebrew prophets into whose race he was born.[2]

There is danger, of course, that we may set up an artificial pattern of the prophet and of prophetic religion and then try to make every prophet fit the pattern. This danger may be averted by constantly remembering that the great prophets were real individuals and that each had his characteristic emphases. Yet it should appear that their similarities are more important than their differences.

[1] *The Hibbert Journal*, XXVIII (1929-30), 102.

[2] For two recent studies discussing Jesus as prophet, see P. E. Davies, "Jesus and the Rôle of the Prophet," *Journal of Biblical Literature*, LXIV (1945), 241-54; and David E. Adams, *Man of God* (New York: Harper, 1941).

The prophetic movement in Israel began in the middle of the eleventh century B.C., when Samuel and Saul flourished. Before this time there were a few individuals who are referred to in later literature as prophets, and there may have been a few sporadic instances of men who were really prophets in the technical sense. Abraham is termed a prophet (Gen. 20:7) by the writer known to scholars as the Elohist, who lived probably in the eighth century B.C. This designation is significant as showing that the Elohist considered a prophet to be one who makes intercession for another. Abimelech is bidden to restore Sarah to Abraham in order that the patriarch may intercede for him with Yahweh and thus save his life. Moses is designated as prophet in Deut. 18:15 and 34:10. This designation of him may go back to Hosea (12:13), and it reveals that the prophets were proud to claim Moses as one of their own. He was a man who spoke for God in a very special sense, but his place in Israelite tradition is more firmly that of leader and lawgiver. Moses' sister, Miriam, is called a prophetess in Exod. 15:20, perhaps because later writers thought of her as an ecstatic dancer. In the book of Judges, Deborah (4:4) and Gideon (6:8)[3] are singled out to be called prophets, probably because they were thought to be more fully endowed with spirit than other judges. All these references seem to reflect merely the judgment of later times.

In the time of Samuel and Saul, however, a genuine prophetic movement began to flourish among the Israelites. The prophets who made up the movement and their successors up to the time of the great prophets may, for purposes of discussion, be divided into several types, but the classification is somewhat artificial and there is considerable overlapping in the types.

Some early prophets were engaged in soothsaying or fortune-telling, being endowed with what was considered second sight. The Israelites called them "seers." The most famous name known to

---

[3] It is not certain that the prophet of Judg. 6:8 is Gideon, but, because of the close connection with the account of Gideon which follows in 6:11 ff., it seems entirely possible.

us in this type is Samuel. The nature of their profession can be conjectured from the fact that Saul and his servant repaired to Samuel in the hope that he might help them locate Saul's father's asses, which they had been unable to find by natural means (I Sam. 9:5-9). That such a profession was not highly regarded may be inferred from the biblical statement that Saul's servant, rather than Saul himself, knew about Samuel and suggested turning to him. We should note, however, that Samuel was also a priest. In this early period the dividing line between priest and prophet was not sharply drawn. There were probably many "seers" in early Israel, and the profession of fortune-telling among the prophets may have lasted for a long time, but we do not find the great prophets indulging in it.

Some of the early prophets were ecstatic. Among them was counted Saul, according to the most revealing passage as to the nature of the ecstatic prophets (I Sam. 10:5-12). After Samuel had privately anointed Saul as king, he gave instructions and told what would happen to him. He said that Saul would come to the hill of God and there meet a band of prophets coming down from a high place, with various musical instruments in their hands, and that they would be "prophesying." "Then the spirit of the Lord will suddenly seize you, and you will prophesy with them and will be changed into another man" (vs. 6). Events came to pass as Samuel had predicted, and this incident gave rise—so popular tradition said—to the proverb: "Is Saul also among the prophets?" This incident reveals several elements that frequently went into ecstatic behavior: the influence of mass contagion, the use of musical instruments, erratic behavior which could be described as being "changed into another man," and the apparently low repute of the ecstatics which could lead the masses to be surprised that Saul was associated with them. We see also the theological interpretation of the phenomenon as "the spirit of the Lord"—or, elsewhere, "the hand of the Lord"—coming upon the prophet.

It is significant that the same Hebrew word is used to describe the actions—and presumably also the speaking—of the prophets on this occasion, the mad raving of Saul against David in his fits of jealousy (I Sam. 18:10), and the highly emotional frenzy of the Baalistic prophets in their conflict with Elijah on Mount Carmel (I Kings 18:29). To translate the word uniformly as "prophesy" gives a false impression; we should perhaps render it "behave ecstatically." The "spirit of the Lord" was thought of as producing both the behavior of Saul in I Sam. 10 and his mad raving against David, except that in the latter case it was an evil spirit from Yahweh.

We would say today that ecstasy was an experience in which the subject lost normal volition and thought—to a greater or less degree —and came under the influence of suggestion from without. There is little detailed information about how the ecstatics acted or what they said. Some descriptions imply great nervous activity, while others suggest a cataleptic state, such as that in which Saul is said to have fallen down and lain naked all day and all night (I Sam. 19:24). Undoubtedly many of the prophets before Amos were ecstatic. Whether the great prophets from Amos on were subject to ecstatic seizure is uncertain. Old Testament scholars now tend to deny that they were. A reasonable judgment seems to be that, although they were not usually subject to abnormal psychological experiences, the great prophets occasionally experienced mild forms of ecstasy, particularly in the visions in which they were commissioned to prophesy.

The "sons of the prophets" are another type known in the age before Amos. These were members of prophetic guilds, each organized under a head, with its members living a somewhat communal existence. These guilds may be roughly compared with monastic orders, but the members did not practice celibacy (II Kings 4:1). They were probably subject to ecstasy, and we may infer that they made their living by telling fortunes, performing miracles, and the like. Elisha was the head of a group of these prophets (II Kings 4:38-41; 6:1-7). There are hints that these men may have worn a distinctive garb, and may even have been branded with identifying marks.

Many of the early prophets were associated in one way or another with the royal court. The kings of Israel frequently, if not always, retained at their courts prophets who were commanded to consult the oracles on important occasions, particularly at the beginning of military campaigns. Such prophets were apparently very numerous. It is recorded, for instance, that Ahab and Jehoshaphat summoned four hundred before attempting a military venture (I Kings 22). From this incident and others of similar nature it appears that most of the court prophets were servile flatterers, telling their king what they believed he wanted to hear. But certain of them were of independent mind, some actually fomenting revolts against existing regimes. Nathan had the boldness to rebuke David for the murder of Uriah and the taking of Bathsheba (II Sam. 12:1-15), and later he was involved with Bathsheba in the plot which secured the throne for Solomon (I Kings 1). Elijah—who was, however, not technically a court prophet—condemned Ahab for the murder of Naboth (I Kings 21). Ahijah was apparently connected with the revolution of Jeroboam (I Kings 11:29-39), and Elisha backed, or even inspired, the revolt of Jehu (II Kings 9).

So we see that the prophets before Amos were of several varieties. Some were members of organized groups, while others were pronounced individualists. Some were sycophants and timeservers, while others were courageous enough to sit in judgment upon kings. Some were highly regarded in their generation, while others were objects of contempt and suspicion. Many were ecstatic, while others —like Elijah—may have been consciously opposed to ecstasy. Among these early prophets are a few—notably Samuel, Nathan, Micaiah ben Imlah (I Kings 22), and Elijah—who prepared the way for the independent, morality-centered careers of the great prophets. Of these Elijah is the greatest of the early prophets, standing for wholehearted service to Israel's God at a time when Queen Jezebel was on the point of substituting the worship of Baal for the religion of Yahweh.

CHAPTER II

THE GREAT PROPHETS

AMOS

THE FIRST OF THE GREAT PROPHETS WAS AMOS OF TEKOA, A SHEPHERD and dresser of sycamore trees who, while denying that he was a professional prophet, helped to give new meaning to the word "prophet." He was in many respects the most uncompromising, the most radical, and the clearest thinking of all the great prophets. He was a pioneer, blazing a daring path for his successors to follow.

The book of Amos is the easiest to read and study of all the prophetic books to be considered. The Hebrew text is generally in good order and is not difficult to translate and interpret. Most of the book is the authentic work of the eighth-century prophet, the only important exceptions being the hopeful appendix with which the book now ends, 9:11-15, and the doxologies of 4:13; 5:8; 9:5-6, inserted to make the thought of the prophet harmonize with that of Job and Second Isaiah.[1] The oracle against Judah in 2:4-5 is also of doubtful authenticity.

Amos possessed fine poetic ability, to a degree which may surprise us in a man of his background. Many of his figurative expressions, drawn from his own experience, are quite vivid. His only public appearance definitely recorded was at Bethel in the northern kingdom (7:10-17). We do not know whether his book represents this one public appearance or is composed of excerpts from a number of oracles delivered in various cities. The latter appears more probable. In its present form the book of Amos is well organized, but we do not know whether it was put together by the prophet himself or by one of his disciples. At any rate, the thought of Amos is original, incisive, and revolutionary.

[1] For a brief discussion of the way secondary material came to be added to prophetic books, see pp. 97-98.

Hosea

Hosea, the immediate successor and possibly for a time the contemporary of Amos, was a man of very different temperament; and
the study of his book presents to the modern reader many difficult
problems. Some of these are incapable of final solution with the
materials we now possess. The first problem confronting the reader
is that of properly translating the Hebrew text. In the form in which
it has come down to us the text of Hosea is frequently corrupt and
sometimes cannot be satisfactorily translated at all. This situation is
due in part, no doubt, to the accidents of time which have occurred in
the transmission of the text; but it may be due also to the prophet's
style, which seems to reflect a temperament highly emotional, sensitive, and restless. In some verses the modern scholar can gain help
from one or more of the ancient versions, but he is sometimes at
a loss to establish a correct text and thus finds accurate translation
and interpretation out of the question.

The reader of Hosea is faced also with the task of interpreting the
first three chapters and relating them to the rest of the book. These
opening chapters are obviously biographical, giving the only direct
information in the book concerning the prophet's personal life. But
how are they to be interpreted? Are they vision, allegory, or history?
Most modern scholars would reply that they are history, relating
Hosea's marital experience, but they would sharply differ on other
questions. Do chapters 1 and 3 refer to the same event, told from
two viewpoints—chapter 1 being in the third person and chapter 3
in the first person—or is chapter 3 a continuation of the first chapter?

The central question, however, in the study of Hosea concerns the
status of his wife, Gomer: Was she a common prostitute, either at
the time of marriage or later, or was she a temple harlot, or was she
a harlot not in any physical sense at all but only in a figurative sense
—that is, religiously or spiritually unfaithful? Almost every conceiv-
able answer has been given to this question, and it is impossible to be
sure of the correct one. The most likely view, which will be elaborat-

ed in the next chapter,[2] is that Gomer was not a harlot at the time of her marriage to Hosea but became unfaithful to him later. Hosea then, in obedience to God's command, determined to continue to love her, just as Yahweh loved Israel in spite of her infidelity.

The book of Hosea originally incorporated oracles directed only to Israel, but an editor of the book has adapted it to Judah. In a few places the word "Judah" has been substituted for "Israel"; most clearly apparent in 12:2, this has occurred also in 5:12, 13, 14; 6:4; 10:11; and possibly 5:10. Lines have been added here and there to adapt the message to Judah, condemnation being expressed in 5:5c; 6:11a; 8:14, and special favor for Judah in 11:12b. Of passages of a hopeful nature, promising future restoration, 1:5, 7; 1:10–2:1; 2:18, 21-23; 3:5; 11:10-11 seem to be secondary. These probably come from the latter part of the Babylonian exile.

In spite of the difficulties involved in studying the book of Hosea, the prophet's main emphases are clear. He stressed (1) the love and mercy of God for Israel and (2) the demand made upon the nation by their God for covenant loyalty and for true knowledge of his nature and will. While Hosea's temperament differed from that of Amos, his message is a wholesome supplement to Amos' insistence on social justice.

ISAIAH OF JERUSALEM

The book of Isaiah is an anthology of prophecy containing materials from many different writers and from many periods of Old Testament history. The nucleus of it is the work of the eighth-century prophet of Jerusalem, Isaiah the son of Amoz, but the portions of this book that may safely be attributed to him constitute not more than one fifth of the total—not more than a dozen chapters altogether. Because of his prominence as a Jerusalem resident, and because he was concerned with hopes for the future more definitely than were former prophets, his book became a depository for many prophetic oracles which he himself did not compose, many of them express-

[2] Pp. 41-43.

ing bright prospects for the future of the nation and of individuals.
We shall consider later the work of the Second Isaiah, found in
chapters 35 and 40-55. Chapters 36-39 are taken with slight change
from II Kings 18:13-20:19. They contain biographical information
concerning Isaiah, but are largely legendary. The genuine words of
the eighth-century prophet are contained chiefly in chapters 1-12 and
28-31. I would assign to Isaiah the following sections of the book
bearing his name, omitting minor glosses: 1:2-31; 2:6-22; 3:1-4:1; 5:1-
30; 6; 7:1-17; 8:1-8, 11-22; 9:8-10:21; 10:28-32; 14:24-31; 17:1-3; 18:1-
6; 20; 22:1-24; 28:1-4, 7-29; 29:1-4, 9-16; 30:1-17; 31:1-4.

Isaiah of Jerusalem lived in the later part of the eighth century
B.C., his public ministry beginning in 742 and continuing to about 700.
He was married and had at least two children. The whole of his
public life was spent in the Judaean capital, and his outlook is dis-
tinctly urban. He was an adviser to the kings of Judah, but the oft-
repeated assertion that he was a member of the nobility is without
a shred of evidence. The fact that he was listened to by kings—although they may not have acted on his advice—indicates only that
he was a prophet in the tradition of Nathan and Micaiah ben Imlah,
not that he was born an aristocrat.

Isaiah was a courageous prophet whose position gave him wider
influence than either Amos or Hosea could command. He was a
good poet, his work comparing favorably with the best of Amos'.
He was not as daring and original in his thinking as Amos, nor as
tender in emotion as Hosea, but his religious ideas were more con-
structive than theirs. In his eyes the greatest sin was pride, and the
great demand made by God upon men was for faith and trust in
his power. In his doctrine of the remnant that would repent and
be preserved by Yahweh he expressed a clearer hope than earlier
prophets had shown, and this doctrine proved to be one of the most
fruitful of all prophetic ideas.

MICAH

Micah was a younger contemporary of Isaiah. It is probable that
he wrote only the first three chapters of the book which now bears

his name (except 2:12-13). Verses 6-8 of the sixth chapter are the finest summary of prophetic ideals found in the Old Testament; they may have been written by Micah, but to deny them to him does not lessen their value.

Micah lived in a little village in southwestern Palestine, Moresheth-Gath, and his viewpoint is constantly that of the peasant. He condemned the sins of city life, his denunciations of social wrongs being in the tradition established by Amos. He did not hesitate to point out the sins of false leaders, including prophets, priests, and princes. The few fragments of his work that survive show us a true prophet, courageous in his preaching and possessed of literary skill.

JEREMIAH

Jeremiah was the great prophet of the seventh century B.C. and the opening decades of the sixth. He is the best known of the prophets, for we have more authentic material concerning Jeremiah than concerning any other single character of the Old Testament, with the possible exception of David. Jeremiah's activities are rather fully related in the biographical and autobiographical portions of the book, which come in part from the pen of Baruch, his secretary. His inner life is well revealed in the peculiarly intimate "confessions" contained in his book (8:18–9:9; 11:18-23; 12:1-6; 15:10-21; 17:9-10, 14-18; 18:18-23; 20:7-12), which portray an introspective nature rarely found among Old Testament writers outside of the psalmists.

It is necessary to add, however, that many of the problems connected with the literary analysis of the book of Jeremiah are exceedingly difficult. There is little reason to doubt the commonly accepted opinion that the first edition of this book was produced by Baruch as his second scroll, as recounted in detail in chapter 36. But there are few objective criteria by which to determine what constituted this first edition. It seems certain that the book of Jeremiah has come to us through the hands of several editors. The first was Baruch, who may not always have reproduced the words of his master verbatim. Others were editors imbued with the spirit of the Deuteronomic school.[3] Still others were exilic and postexilic eschatologists who wished to make the words of Jeremiah more hopeful. We need not list all the passages of this book which are secondary, but the more important sections which must be excluded from Jeremiah's writings are the following: much of chapter 10, influenced by Second Isaiah and late psalmists; 11:1-8, a Deuteronomic section; 17:19-27, concerned with Sabbath observance, probably from the time of Nehemiah; much of chapters 30, 31, and 33, where the brightest promises of restoration have been collected; and the oracles against foreign nations in 46:13-51:64.

In spite of the great amount of material available for understanding Jeremiah, there is perhaps no other Old Testament personality who has been the object of so much popular misconception. He is generally thought of as the "weeping prophet" and the pessimist par excellence. This reputation comes largely from the fact that the book of Lamentations is ascribed to him. It can easily be demonstrated, however, that this book was not written by Jeremiah. It is true that Jeremiah could on occasion weep (9:1), but he probably did not weep any oftener than Jesus of Nazareth. And, like Jesus, he wept for the sins and sufferings of others, not for himself.

It is much more accurate to think of Jeremiah as a man of varying moods. There were occasions when he entered the Slough of Despond and even cursed the day of his birth (20:14-18); but on other occasions he felt so strong and courageous that he compared himself to a fortified city, an iron pillar, and a bronze wall against the whole of the land (1:18). He could question God in a very intimate way (12:1), and even feel that his God had "duped" him (20:7); but he could also say that the words of God were to him a source of great joy and delight (15:16).

In his external life the chief characteristic of Jeremiah was his courage. The biographical portions of his book show that, however much he might have been torn by internal struggles, he was always

[3] For details see my article "Jeremiah and Deuteronomy," *Journal of Near Eastern Studies*, I (1942), 156-73.

outwardly courageous, persistent, and loyal to his deepest convictions. He paid for his courage on more than one occasion by arrest and imprisonment, and almost with his life. How far he was on such occasions from the "weeping prophet" of popular misconception! We must also deny that he was a pessimist. A true historical perspective reveals that Jeremiah was a realist—a religious realist, daring to speak boldly to superficial optimists.

The importance of Jeremiah in the history of Hebrew religion is due not so much to his original ideas or his literary ability as to his character and personality. In his thinking he built on the foundations laid by his predecessors, especially Hosea, and his most original and profound religious idea was his teaching of the "new covenant," expressed in 31:31-34. His literary ability is somewhat obscured by the prose style of Baruch, but some of his poems are of very high quality.

Jeremiah is sometimes referred to as the father of personal religion, or the father of true prayer, or the connecting link between the older prophets and the psalmists. He deserves these titles, especially the first. But his contributions to the ideal of personal religion are not so much explicit as implicit in his thought. Even the new covenant is to be a covenant with "the house of Israel and the house of Judah" (31:31), but the idea was bound to break its nationalistic limitations and become the Magna Charta of personal religion. Jeremiah promoted the ideal of personal religion also by his insistence that sin comes primarily from the sinful heart, by his divorce of religion from dependence on the temple and the land of Palestine, and by his own intimate experiences with God.

EZEKIEL

The book of Ezekiel is today the subject of more discussion among Old Testament students than any other prophetic book, and it must be confessed that there is little agreement on its interpretation. A generation ago this book was generally accepted as a unified work, the product of a prophet named Ezekiel who lived in the sixth century B.C., both before and after the fall of Jerusalem in 587 B.C.

The change which has come about in the interpretation of this book is well illustrated by the differences between the first edition of J. M. P. Smith's *The Prophets and Their Times,* published in 1925, and the revised edition of W. A. Irwin, published in 1941. Smith entitled the chapter on Ezekiel "The Father of Judaism," and took the position that the book is what it purports to be. Irwin placed a question mark after Smith's title and rewrote the chapter almost entirely. He considered relatively little of the present book genuine, believing it to be "a cross-section of Jewish piety and teaching through the last five centuries B.C. or perhaps longer" and "not the father, but the child, of Judaism." [4]

The most extreme view regarding Ezekiel was advanced by C. C. Torrey in 1930 in his *Pseudo-Ezekiel and the Original Prophecy.*[5] Torrey believes that the original prophecy (constituting the major portion of the present book) was written near 230 B.C. by a man of priestly rank in the city of Jerusalem, as a pseudepigraph—that is, as a historical novel or an imaginative autobiography—purporting to be from a prophet who lived in the reign of Manasseh in the seventh century B.C. An editor living a short time later than 230 B.C. gave the book its present Babylonian setting by a few ingenious changes and additions here and there. If Torrey's view is correct, there was no prophet named Ezekiel and the work which goes by his name must be classed with the book of Daniel. This theory labors under many difficulties. It is entirely too skeptical and radical, uprooting Ezekiel from a historical background into which he fits and putting him, as regards both the purported date of the prophet and the actual date of the book, into a setting which is not appropriate. Many of Torrey's

---

[4] Pp. 215-16. Irwin has since presented his views of Ezekiel in *The Problem of Ezekiel* (Chicago: University Press, 1943). I believe that Irwin considers too much material as secondary, and that his resultant Ezekiel is not a convincing personality.

[5] "Yale Oriental Series: Researches," Vol. XVIII (New Haven: Yale University Press, 1930).

arguments have been answered in detail,[6] and few Old Testament specialists have adopted his view.

It is difficult, however, to maintain the old view of the book of Ezekiel and consider it essentially unified and authentic. In its present form it presents a figure with too many and too great inconsistencies—in character, thought, and style. Ezekiel is both prophet and priest, and apocalyptist as well. He is represented as holding to both nationalism and individualism. He can on occasion write fine poetry, but he often writes wretched, dull prose. It has usually been found necessary to draw upon abnormal psychology to explain some of his experiences, and it must be confessed that many parts of the book seem to be divorced from real life.

An analysis of the book of Ezekiel which obviates many of the difficulties has been made by I. G. Matthews.[7] He sees in the book three strata of material: (a) The authentic messages of the sixth-century prophet, from a man who lived in or near Jerusalem both before and after the fall of that city. He may have been a native of the northern kingdom. It is not clear whether he was ever in Babylonia or not. At any rate he was "a writer with fair literary gifts, delighting in vivid illustration, facile with parable and allegory, with the ethical insight of the earlier prophets, and passionately indignant at the social and religious practices of his people. He was withal a normal, healthy-minded, vigorous prophet, who to his own generation was the unheeded voice of God." [8] (b) The Babylonian setting of the book and many editorial sections, supplied by "The Babylonian Editor," a disciple and interpreter of Ezekiel who lived in the period between 550 and 500 B.C. He put a great deal more emphasis on ritual, the temple, and the law than did the prophet. He

---

[6] See especially S. Spiegel, *Harvard Theological Review,* XXIV (1931), 245-321, and *Journal of Biblical Literature,* LIV (1935), 145-71. Torrey's views are expanded in *Journal of Biblical Literature,* LI (1932), 179-81, and LIII (1934), 291-320.

[7] *Ezekiel* (American commentary on the Old Testament; Philadelphia: American Baptist Publication Society, 1939). Somewhat similar views are held by V. Herntrich, *Ezechielprobleme* (Giessen, 1932); and J. B. Harford, *Studies in the Book of Ezekiel* (New York: Macmillan, 1935).

[8] Matthews, *op. cit.,* p. xxiii.

wrote or edited chapters 40-48, as well as other parts of the book. (c) Many of the curses against foreign nations, and the more developed ritualistic and eschatological portions of the book, supplied by still later editors. Matthews conveniently summarizes the three principal contributors to the book in the following words: "Ezekiel was a mystic, cultivating the inner light; his disciple was a priest, believing in sacramental grace; and the apocalyptist, failing to find God in history, turned expectantly to the age that was to be and put all his hope in the wonder-working God." [9]

Such a view makes of the prophet Ezekiel an intelligible personality and places him in the rank of the great prophets. While it must be admitted that the interpretation suggested by Matthews is by no means the final one, it seems to be right in principle, and has accordingly been accepted in general in the following discussion.

SECOND ISAIAH

The last in the succession of the great Hebrew prophets was the Second Isaiah (or Deutero-Isaiah), in whose thinking the prophetic idea of God and other prophetic conceptions reached their climax. The work of this man is now contained in the latter part of the book of Isaiah. Modern critical scholars are all but unanimously agreed that no part of this book after chapter 39 can possibly be the work of the eighth-century Isaiah of Jerusalem, and the commonly accepted opinion is that chapters 40-55 are the product of an unknown prophet who lived in the latter part of the sixth century B.C. These chapters differ so markedly in vocabulary, style, thought, and historical background from the genuine work of Isaiah of Jerusalem that they must be from someone who lived later than he did, if literary and historical criticism have any validity whatsoever.

There is some difference of opinion as to how much of the present book of Isaiah constitutes the work of the Second Isaiah. A few scholars believe that chapters 40-66 are a unit, and some would pre-

[9] *Ibid.*, p. xxx.

fix to them chapters 34-35.[10] It is impossible, however, to escape the impression that many parts of the last eleven chapters of the book are on a lower plane, in both style and content, than chapters 40-55. I believe that Deutero-Isaiah is the author of chapters 40-55 and probably also chapter 35. It seems likely that chapters 35, 40-48 were written shortly before the fall of Babylon to the army of Cyrus of Persia in 539 B.C., and chapters 49-55 sometime after that event.

The Second Isaiah is the most original and creative thinker among the Old Testament prophets, and he is also a fine poet. His work lacks some of the spontaneity of earlier prophets, but he is more self-consciously a literary artist than any of the others. His thought presents to us the triumph of Hebrew religion over the tragedy of the Babylonian exile, a tragedy which might have resulted in the destruction of the religion of Yahweh. He does not deal with some of the problems which exercised the mind of former prophets, but is primarily concerned with showing that Yahweh is the one and only God and presenting the magnificent portrait of the Servant of the Lord. His book is a prophecy of hope and encouragement, but the author is a true prophet, able to impart hope without compromising prophetic ideals and without descending to a narrow nationalism. No book of the Old Testament presents a higher conception of God or a more universal religious outlook.

These seven are the great prophets of the Old Testament which are used as criteria in evaluating prophetic characteristics. Certain books of the Old Testament which are ordinarily classed as prophecy are not included in our study.

The book of Daniel is found with the prophets in the English Bible, but it is not, properly speaking, a book of prophecy such as the ones we have been considering. It is an apocalypse, comparable to the book of Revelation in the New Testament. In the Hebrew Bible it is not classified with either the Former or the Latter Prophets, but

---

[10] The unity of chaps. 34-35, 40-66 is maintained especially by C. C. Torrey in *The Second Isaiah* (New York: Scribner, 1928), which gives a fine translation and splendid appreciation of those chapters.

among the miscellaneous group called Writings. In a sense the apocalyptists were successors of the prophets, but they constitute a class to themselves.

The books of Jonah and Nahum are somewhat mistakenly classified as prophecies. The former is a short story or parable *about* a prophet named Jonah, not the work *of* Jonah. The book is informed by a very fine spirit, and the author was one of the few men in the postexilic age to catch the universalistic message of Second Isaiah. It is really the unknown author of this little story who is the prophet, rather than Jonah himself. The book of Nahum is largely a triumphant ode over the fall of Nineveh, written sometime near 612 B.C., when that city was taken by the Chaldaeans and Medes. The author is not a true prophet, but a poet. In some respects he was a false prophet. The spirit of hatred of a foreign nation pervading his poetry is alien to the true prophet. Similar judgment must be passed on the little book of Obadiah, which was written after the fall of Jerusalem.

There are two prophets of the pre-exilic age who probably would be considered among the great if we had more of their work: Habakkuk and Zephaniah. As their books now stand, their work is so fragmentary, and the literary and historical problems associated with them so elusive, that it seems best to omit them from our study.

Several books from the postexilic period are omitted from consideration here: Haggai, Zechariah, Malachi, and Joel. These are important books for the study of their age, but their authors are not as great as the prophets of the pre-exilic and exilic ages. They present few new ideas, and some of them show direct literary dependence on the older prophets (Joel, for example). Some of them represent the harmonization or compromise of prophetic and priestly ideas and ideals—for example, Haggai, Zechariah, and Malachi. Failure to include these men among the great prophets should not blind our eyes to their importance. They were doubtless very important in their own time, and it is likely that the spirit of compromise exhibited in their messages was utterly necessary. It may well be true that if they had not done their work well, the work of the greater prophets of former times would not have survived.

Chapter III

THE CALLED OF GOD

"GOD HAS A FEW OF US WHOM HE WHISPERS IN THE EAR," SAYS ROBERT Browning in "Abt Vogler." The prophets were among these few, and they believed they were commissioned to go and cry aloud what God had whispered to them—in the market places, in the temple courts, even from the housetops if necessary. They believed they were verily called of God to speak in his name to his people. A burden was placed upon them which they had to bear, willingly or upon compulsion. They were not self-appointed, but God-chosen. It was not their own will which they sought to do, but God's.

If we would understand the prophets and prophetic religion, we must first try to understand their own conception of their mission and, if possible, accept them in the light of that conception. Their attitude is most obvious in the description of the divine commission, usually accompanied by a vision, which preceded the public career of most of the prophets. The call of Isaiah, of Jeremiah, and of Ezekiel is very clearly described in their respective books. Less clear, but capable of reconstruction, is the commission given to Amos, Hosea, and Second Isaiah. Only about Micah have we no information as to his call. There is an incident in the life of Jesus which may readily be interpreted as his inaugural vision and divine commission.

THE CALL OF ISAIAH

Isaiah received his divine summons to a prophetic career in a vision now preserved in the sixth chapter of his book. It is so clearly and simply written, and contains so many profound ideas, that it has become a classic record of an experience of this type.

The vision came to Isaiah as he was in the temple, no doubt in the court of the real temple in Jerusalem, and not in an imaginary

heavenly temple. As a layman he was not within the temple sanctuary itself, to which only priests had access, but in the outer court.
But there Isaiah saw and heard much more than the thousands
of ordinary worshipers who came to make their offerings and
raise their prayers. He had a vision of the Lord in majesty and
holiness: he saw the Lord "seated on a throne, lofty and uplifted,
with his skirts filling the temple." This majestic being was sur-
rounded and ministered to by six-winged seraphs who chanted
antiphonally:

> Holy, holy, holy is the Lord of hosts!
> The fullness of the whole earth is his glory!

This vision of the holy and lofty Deity, with the accompanying
tremor and smoke, led him to a sense of his own impurity and
unworthiness, and he cried out:

> Woe is me! Surely I am undone,
>   For a man of unclean lips am I,
> And among a people of unclean lips
>   Do I dwell.
> For it is the King, the Lord of hosts,
>   Mine eyes have seen!

His realization and confession of sin led immediately to the divine
forgiveness, symbolized by that part of the vision in which a seraph
took a glowing hot stone from the altar and touched his lips with it,
at the same time pronouncing forgiveness.

After this purification Isaiah heard the voice of the Lord asking:

> Whom shall I send,
> And who will go for us?

The prophet's response was immediate: "Here am I: send me!" The
divine summons then came to him to go and say to his fellow
Israelites:

> Hear indeed, but understand not!
> And see indeed, but perceive not!

The result of Isaiah's prophecy was expressed in the following words:

> Make fat the mind of this people,
> Make heavy their ears,
>   And smear over their eyes;
> Lest they see with their eyes,
> And hear with their ears,
>   And their minds understand,
> And they repent, and be healed!

This must have seemed strange to Isaiah, but his only response was to ask, "How long, O Lord?" To this question the answer came:

> Until they lie waste:
>   Cities without inhabitant,
> And houses without man,
>   And the ground be left desolate;
> And the Lord remove man far away,
>   And the forsaken places in the land be many:
> Even if a tenth remain in it,
>   It must still be destroyed! [1]

This initial vision and commission of the prophet Isaiah is clear and requires little interpretation until one comes to verse 9. From that verse to the end of the chapter the commands laid upon the prophet seem too harsh for utterance by a holy God, and it is hard to understand how a prophet would be willing to undertake a task which was announced to be hopeless from the beginning. In fact, as the words stand they appear to say that the preaching of the prophet will have the effect of condemning the people, making dull their whole being and rendering them incapable of repentance.

[1] The rest of vs. 13, which is too corrupt for satisfactory translation, seems to be largely a secondary gloss.

Most commentators have expressed the belief that the sixth chapter of Isaiah was not written down immediately after the experience to which it refers, but some years later, or even near the close of Isaiah's career. It may well be true that the chapter was not written down immediately, but only after a few years of experience; yet the vividness of the whole scene makes it improbable that Isaiah waited until the end of his life to write or dictate it. Furthermore, the idea expressed in verse 13 concerning the "tenth"—if the above translation is correct—is opposed to Isaiah's developed doctrine of the "remnant." It is not necessary to take refuge in the theory that this chapter expresses the prophet's later disillusionment after many unhappy experiences in prophesying. Without taking these words too literally, we may see in them the great depths of Isaiah's conviction and his devotion to his prophetic mission. What he is attempting to say through verses 9-13 is that he is willing to go and preach to his people *even if* they do not pay any attention to him, and *if* the only result of his work is that the land will nevertheless be destroyed. Isaiah, like every true prophet, did not wish his work to be measured by pragmatic tests. He cared little whether his counsel was heeded by man or not. He cared only that he should do faithfully what the Lord commanded him to do, and that men should know a prophet had been in their midst.

THE CALL OF JEREMIAH

Jeremiah's call is as clear as that of Isaiah, but it presents a number of new ideas and reveals a personality far different from Isaiah's. Jeremiah's commission is recorded in the first chapter of his book.

We do not know the circumstances in which Jeremiah received his call, but he too had a vision and heard the Lord speaking. He was at first overwhelmed with a sense of being divinely predetermined for his mission from the earliest possible time, as he heard God speak:

> Before I formed you in the womb, I knew you,
> And before you were born, I sanctified you;
> A prophet to the nations have I appointed you.

Jeremiah's immediate response was not to volunteer and gladly take up his mission, as Isaiah had done; but, like Moses in a similar situation (Exod. 3:11 ff., 6:30 ff.), he was overcome by a sense of his own unworthiness and inability: "Alas, O Lord God! Behold, I am not eloquent, for I am but a child!" To this protest he received the reply:

> Say not, "I am but a child,"
> For unto whomsoever I shall send you, you shall go,
>   And whatsoever I command you, you shall speak;
> Be not afraid of them,
>   For I am with you to deliver you.

Then in a vision Jeremiah saw God stretch forth his hand and touch him upon the lips and say:

> Behold, I have put my words in your mouth;
>   See, I have appointed you today
> Over nations and over kingdoms,
>   To pull down and uproot,[2] to build and plant.

Jeremiah then received two specific visions. The first was of an object which the prophet identified as an almond rod. The reply of God was: "You have correctly seen, for I watch over my word to perform it." The significance of this vision is not immediately apparent, especially when read in any language other than the original Hebrew. But it is quite obvious in the Hebrew that there is a play on words, or pun, of the type frequently met in the Old Testament. The word for almond is *shāqēd,* and the word meaning "watch over," in the form necessary here, is *shōqēd.* But there is probably an even deeper meaning. In the light of a number of Old Testament passages which mention a rod or rods (such as Num. 17:1-11; Ezek. 7:10; Eccles. 12:5; Zech. 11:7, 10, 14) it is probable that the almond rod is here a symbol of the judgment of the Lord

---

[2] The words "to destroy and to overthrow" in Hebrew are probably not original, having been added under the influence of verses such as 18:7 and 24:6. They are superfluous and overload the meter.

against a rebellious people.[3] The vision means, therefore, that the Lord has pronounced judgment against the people of Israel because of their sins against him, and he is about to bring their punishment upon them. He chooses Jeremiah as his mouthpiece to announce the coming judgment.

The final vision of Jeremiah is of a "seething caldron, with its mouth facing from the north." The significance of it is that "from the north shall misfortune be blown upon all the inhabitants of the land." The purpose of this vision is only to point out the direction from which God is about to bring punishment upon the Israelites for their rebellion against him. There are a number of passages, undoubtedly spoken in the beginning of his prophetic career, in which Jeremiah vividly announces the coming of a people "from the north" to bring ruin upon the land. Scholars have usually identified this peril from the north with the Scythians, but it is more probable that the prophet had in mind that alliance of Medes and Chaldaeans which brought about the fall of Nineveh in 612 b.c.[4] The Chaldaeans did eventually, in 587 b.c., destroy Jerusalem and exile many Jews.

Jeremiah's call and commission are unusual in a number of respects: the emphasis on the prophet's having been predestined to his task even from conception; his appointment as a prophet not simply to the Israelites but "to the nations"; and his hesitation, which contrasts strongly with Isaiah's action in immediately volunteering. There is no prophet, however, who had so overpowering a sense of being called to his prophetic mission as Jeremiah. He was of a shy, reticent, and introspective disposition, and was deeply grieved by the lack of response to his words spoken in the name of God. But he could not keep from prophesying, for he felt an inner compulsion to continue regardless of his own feelings and the unfavorable response of the people.

[3] See P. S. Wood, "Jeremiah's Figure of the Almond Rod," *Journal of Biblical Literature*, LXI (1942), 99-103.

[4] For details see my article "The Peril from the North in Jeremiah," *Journal of Biblical Literature*, LIX (1940), 499-513.

The inner conflicts which he suffered are nowhere more vividly depicted than in 20:7-9:

> Thou, O Lord, hast duped me, and I let myself be duped!
> Thou hast been stronger than I, and hast prevailed!
> I have become a laughingstock the whole day long;
> Everyone mocks me!
> For as often as I speak, I cry out;
> "Violence and destruction!" I preach;
> Because the word of the Lord has become for me
> A reproach and derison the whole day long.
> If I say, "I will forget him,
> And not again speak in his name,"
> Then there is in my heart as it were a burning fire
> Shut up within my bones;
> And I am wearied by holding it in—
> I cannot endure it!

THE CALL OF EZEKIEL

Ezekiel's call to a prophet's career, as recorded in the first three chapters of his book, is more difficult to interpret than those of Isaiah and Jeremiah. In its present form the call and its accompanying visions are extremely prolix and intricate, and have given rise to highly imaginative speculations. It seems likely, however, that the original account of this prophet's vision and commission was brief and vivid, but has been obscured by prosaic and weird additions of later editors.

It may be that Ezekiel's experience was actually somewhat as follows. As he was standing in a valley near Jerusalem (3:22-23), he beheld a great storm in the north. It was a violent storm, accompanied by a heavy wind and lightning flashes, but at its end the sun broke through and a beautiful rainbow appeared. This physical storm soon melted into an ecstatic vision in which Ezekiel saw the holy and majestic God seated upon a throne, borne aloft above a crystal dome, which in turn was borne by four living creatures (1:4-5, 22, 26-28). He then heard the voice of God speaking to him from the throne, announcing that he would send Ezekiel as a prophet to the rebellious house of Israel. He was told that they would be stiffhearted and would refuse to hearken to him, but he was nevertheless to be a true prophet (2:3-7; 3:4-9). God declared that he would give to Ezekiel his word and message, which was symbolized by a written scroll offered the prophet with the command that he should eat it (2:8–3:3). This meant not that he was to study the scriptures which had been written before his day but that his message was truly placed in his mouth by the majestic God. At the same time, or a little later, Ezekiel felt that he was appointed as a watchman to the Israelites, to warn them of their impending danger (3:16-21).

The similarity between the visions of Ezekiel and Isaiah has often been noted. Both men had a vision of a God of majesty and holiness, both received a divine commission to prophesy, and both were warned that the people would pay scant heed to their words. But Ezek. 1–3 is not just a literary expansion of the sixth chapter of Isaiah. There are enough original elements in these chapters to show that Ezekiel's experience was vivid and real.

The Call of Amos

The call to a prophetic ministry of Amos, the earliest of the literary prophets, is not presented to us in as clear and obvious a fashion as those of the prophets just discussed, but it can be reconstructed with considerable confidence. It seems probable that the four visions recorded in Amos 7:1-9; 8:1-2 actually came to the prophet while he was still in his native town "following the flock" (7:15), and that they were to him the summons to a prophetic career which took him northward to Bethel. In each of these visions Amos has a natural experience which leads to a vision with a religious meaning.[5]

[5] My discussion of these visions owes much to Julian Morgenstern, *Amos Studies* (Cincinnati: Hebrew Union College Press, 1941), I, 52-114, although it does not agree with that study in all details.

The first of these experiences came to the shepherd in the spring "at the beginning of the coming up of the aftergrowth." As he was walking across the countryside he came upon some locusts, perhaps in large number, and began to imagine what tremendous damage they could do if unchecked. Then, as his imagination soared, he saw a great plague of locusts, fashioned by Yahweh himself, which were about to consume the herbage of the land completely. This vision was to him a symbol of the wrath of God which was about to destroy his land and people, and Amos prayed: "O my Lord, Yahweh, forgive! How can Jacob endure, for he is small?" In response to this prayer God revoked his purpose and said, "It shall not be!"

Again a few months later a second vision came to Amos. It was at the height of summer, and he had observed the severe midsummer heat withering the grass and crops, drying up springs, and causing much suffering. This natural experience led him to another vision in which he saw Yahweh summoning a great supernatural fire to destroy the whole land; it had already consumed the subterranean ocean—"the great deep"—and was on the point of devouring also the land. Again Amos prayed: "O my Lord, Yahweh, desist! How can Jacob endure, for he is small?" A second time Yahweh revoked his purpose and stayed his hand of judgment.

The third vision came sometime later, but the season of the year is not of special significance. The Tekoan shepherd this time must have seen a wall which was not straight but out of plumb. This object passed over into a vision in which he saw Yahweh standing by a wall with a plumb line in his hand. This became a symbol that God was about to measure Israel as with a plumb line and, finding it not straight but crooked, was about to destroy the nation. If Amos prayed this time on behalf of his fellow countrymen, the reply was different from what he had received in the two former visions. The verdict now was: "I will not pass by them again!"

The final vision came at the end of the fall harvest. It was the time when freshly gathered summer fruit was heaped up in baskets. The shepherd saw these baskets, and one in particular must have struck him with special force. As he mulled over the name for "summer fruit"—*qayits* in Hebrew—he had a final vision. This time he heard God saying:

> The end [*qēts*] has come upon my people Israel,
> I will not pass by them again!

The use of a pun, or play on words, in this vision may strike the English reader strangely. While we may consider the pun as the lowest form of wit—unless *we* happen to think of the pun ourselves! —there is abundant evidence that a play on words was highly regarded by the Hebrews, and significant messages are often contained in puns such as the one here.

After experiencing these visions Amos heard God say to him: "Go, prophesy to my people Israel!" (7:15). So he went to the Israelite town of Bethel, apparently at the moment of some great religious festival, possibly New Year's Day (in the autumn), as Julian Morgenstern has suggested. He selected an occasion when abundant sacrifices were being offered to present his scorching denunciation of dependence on ritual instead of righteousness. Of course, as pointed out above, we do not know whether Amos made only this one public appearance at Bethel or prophesied several times, both there and at other cities in the northern kingdom.

It is important to notice that with Amos, as with Isaiah and other prophets, many of the most significant elements of his message are contained or implied in his opening visions. Here we see Amos' belief in Yahweh as a deity who is concerned with the whole world as well as with his chosen people, who is both a God of mercy, ready at first to forgive his people when Amos entreats for them, and of justice, ready to visit punishment when they pass beyond the possibility of real repentance. It is well to remember that the God of Amos is not wholly a stern God of cold justice. In the first two visions he responds to Amos' prayer with a promise of forgiveness.

THE CALL OF HOSEA

The book of Amos' successor, Hosea, does not tell of a well-defined call to a prophetic career, and the details of Hosea's life are hidden in considerable obscurity. The first three chapters, which seem to be biographical, have been subjected to widely divergent interpretations. Nevertheless, it is probable that within them we can discern the summons to prophesy, or at least the moment which made Hosea a distinctive prophet.

As the result partly of recent discoveries regarding the religion of the Canaanites among whom the Israelites lived in Palestine, some scholars have of late maintained that Hosea's wife, Gomer, was a sacred harlot, a religious prostitute connected with one of the temples. There can be no doubt that harlots of this kind existed in the religion of ancient Canaan, and that the Hebrews at times allowed them even in their own religion. W. A. Irwin believes not only that Gomer was a temple prostitute but that Hosea contracted a second marriage with a woman who was undeniably a bad woman, an adulteress.[6] The latter belief he derives from chapter 3.

Two considerations compel us to oppose the view that Gomer was a temple harlot. The first is the fact that the Hebrew word used to describe her in 1:2 is not the word for temple harlot. The Hebrews had a special word to denote such a person—*qedēshāh*. It is used in Deut. 23:17 and Gen. 38:21-22; and Hosea himself knew it, for he used it once in 4:14. Had he, or an editor of his book, wished to say that Gomer was a temple harlot, he would have employed this word. The phrase used to describe Gomer actually is *'ēsheth zenūnīm*, literally "woman of harlotries." This phrase would most naturally be understood as describing a woman who was unchaste in some abstract sense.

[6] See his revision of J. M. P. Smith's *The Prophets and Their Times* (Chicago: University of Chicago Press, 1941) pp. 70-76.

The second consideration involves a question which undeniably will be answered variously by different people. Would it be possible for Hosea, or any other prophet, to marry a harlot—either a temple harlot or a common whore—even under what he felt to be the command of God, and then condemn harlotry as he does in 4:13-14 and elsewhere in his prophecies? The prophets of Israel did and said things which we consider peculiar, but no other prophet is represented as doing something patently immoral for the sake of his message.

Considering everything, we seem to find the fewest difficulties in the following view: Hosea married Gomer at a time when she was not a known harlot of any kind, though she was—as we shall see— potentially a harlot and could, therefore, be called an 'ēsheth zenūnīm. Hosea probably loved Gomer and at the time of marriage considered her to be a pure woman. He lived happily with her for a time, prophesying to Israel largely messages of doom and destruction. Three children born to the union were given prophetic names indicative of the relationship between Yahweh and Israel and having nothing to do with the relationship between Hosea and Gomer. But after the birth of the third child Hosea discovered Gomer's infidelity; when it began we do not know. The second chapter expresses in part his reflections upon making this discovery, interwoven with reflections on the relation of Israel to Yahweh. Hosea decided to treat his wife as any adulteress of the time was supposed to be treated— expel her and allow her to be killed (2:3). But then there came to him the command of Yahweh: "Go and *still* love a woman beloved of her paramour and an adulteress, as Yahweh loves Israel, though they turn unto other gods and love raisin cakes" (3:1).[7] He obeyed this command, but whether or not he truly won Gomer back we do not know. When later he wrote down or dictated his experiences, he had come to the conclusion that in the very beginning Yahweh

---

[7] Cf. J. A. Bewer, "The Story of Hosea's Marriage," *American Journal of Semitic Languages*, XXII (1905-6), 120-30. My interpretation largely agrees with Bewer's.

had commanded him to marry "a woman of harlotries," for Gomer was potentially a harlot at the time of marriage.

This interpetation of Hosea's domestic life considers the command of 3:1 as the crucial moment in his career. While not actually the initial summons to a prophet's mission, it was the moment which gave him a distinctive belief and message—namely, that Yahweh had loved Israel in the desert period and continued to love Israel in spite of her infidelity, just as Hosea believed it his divine duty to continue to love Gomer. It was a moment which also gave him an insight into his past life that enabled him to interpet his marriage to Gomer as obedience to divine decree. It turned Hosea from a prophet of doom to a prophet of hope and redemption.

THE CALL OF SECOND ISAIAH

The last of the Hebrew prophets whose commission concerns us, Second Isaiah, is known only through his own writings. We have no biographical information about him, and nowhere does he tell us clearly of his call to prophesy; but we may with some assurance reconstruct it from what we know of his historical background and message, and from a brief hint in Isa. 40:6-8.

This anonymous prophet lived in the sixth century B.C., when the Jews were suffering under the Babylonian captivity. Whether he lived in Palestine or in Babylonia—or perhaps both—is not known, but he must have been aware of the conditions of his people. Many of them had been deported to Babylonia, and, while the Babylonians were not cruel masters, the exiles longed for home. Those who were left in Palestine were in a land which had been overrun by the Babylonian invaders. Their temple was partially destroyed, and they were under foreign government. Worst of all, the defeat of Jews by Babylonians must have seemed to many to indicate the defeat of the Jewish deity, Yahweh, by the Babylonian Marduk!

The sensitive man whom we call Second Isaiah pondered deeply the condition of his fellow men, the religion he had been taught, and the world situation. He was probably a young man when a

Persian named Cyrus, living in an obscure corner of the world, Anshan, was beginning to embark upon a career of world conquest. He saw Cyrus make himself master of all Persia, and then (547 B.C.) defeat Croesus of Lydia, the monarch of storied wealth. Slowly there seems to have come to Second Isaiah the conviction that this Cyrus was to be the instrument, or one of the instruments, for the redemption of Israel. Cyrus, a strong man in a weak world, was remarkably tolerant in matters of religion. Second Isaiah was later to term him the "shepherd" of the Lord, the "anointed" of Yahweh (Isa. 44:28; 45:1). In due time this prophet came to believe that he could preach comfort to his people, true comfort based on a universal monotheism, without compromising prophetic ideals.

Isa. 40:6-8 gives a brief glimpse into what may have constituted the decisive call of Second Isaiah. While not a vision, it does seem to have involved hearing a voice. It is perhaps more soliloquy, debate with himself, than conversation with God; but it gave Second Isaiah the courage to embark upon his prophetic mission. In 40:6 we read that he heard "the voice of one saying, 'Cry!'" And he said in reply,

> What shall I cry?
> All flesh is grass,
>   And all its endurance as the flower of the field.
> The grass withers, the flower fades,
>   When the breath of the Lord breathes upon it.

But then there came back the answer:

> The grass withers, the flower fades,
>   But the word of our God shall abide forever!

In the conviction that the word of God is eternal and abiding amid the transitory things of "flesh," he began his prophetic ministry, which may have been confined to the written word.

THE CALL OF JESUS

The incident in the life of Jesus which may be interpeted as his inaugural vision and divine commission is his baptism by John the Baptist and the attendant vision and audition. Jesus, attracted by the preaching and ministry of the Baptist, came from his home in Nazareth to the Jordan for the purpose, as Matthew says, of being baptized by John (3:13)—as many others were doing. But Jesus had an experience immediately following his baptism which marked him out clearly from all the others who had come to John. The incident is recounted simply and briefly in Mark 1:10-11: "And straightway, coming up out of the water, he saw the heavens rent asunder, and the Spirit descending upon him like a dove; and a voice came out of the heavens [saying], 'Thou art my beloved Son; in thee I am well pleased.'" This earliest gospel account makes the experience one which came to Jesus alone, whereas some of the later gospels imply that the Spirit was seen and the voice heard by others as well (Luke 3:22; John 1:33). The gospel of Mark is closer to the event. We may well suppose that to Jesus, as to the earlier prophets, this vision was in part a culmination of earlier brooding and observing. In this moment he felt himself chosen as God's representative, his Son, now filled with God's spirit and given courage and strength to sustain him through a career of doing his will and preaching his word. The relationship between him and God was to be, however, much more intimate than that enjoyed by any of the Old Testament prophets; for he was to be, as they were not, the Christ and Redeemer.

THE NATURE OF "THE CALLED OF GOD"

If we pause for a moment to think about the experiences of the prophets at the time of their call or commission, we shall be able to understand better the nature of the prophet.

First, we may note that the prophet was one who had "eyes to see and ears to hear" more than was seen and heard by the common man. Many a Hebrew worshiped at the temple, but only Isaiah saw the Lord in all his majesty there. Amos was not the first man in Tekoa to see locusts, the withering heat of summer, a crooked wall, or baskets of summer fruit; but he saw in these simple things meanings which were hidden from others. To Jeremiah the twig of an almond tree became of special significance, and a storm to Ezekiel. Hosea through his marriage learned more about God's nature than any other of his day.

In noting that the prophet saw unusual significance in common things and events, we do not wish to deny that their experiences were governed by God or that they were in the best sense supernatural. But we should understand that the ancient Hebrew did not make so sharp a distinction as we make between the natural and the supernatural. To him his entire life and his whole world were supernatural in that they were governed by God. He believed that God had customary and usual ways of dealing with his world and with life, but he did not deny that God could and frequently did deal with man in unusual and extraordinary ways. The prophets were men with whom God dealt in an unusual manner, manifesting himself to a degree not vouchsafed to ordinary mortals. One of his ways of expressing himself to the prophets was to open their eyes and minds to see and understand significance and meaning in ordinary things.

Another fact which should strike us in thinking of these experiences is the importance in most of them of the prophet's *mouth* and of the *word* of God. Isaiah feels that he is a man of unclean lips living among people of unclean lips. The seraph cleanses only his mouth, but then he feels pure enough to volunteer for God's work. Jeremiah is told, "Behold, I put my words in your mouth." Ezekiel is given a scroll to eat. Second Isaiah comes to the conviction that in spite of the transitoriness of human flesh the word of God must stand forever.

In a very revealing passage (15:19) Jeremiah hears God say to him:

> If you will repent, then I shall restore you;
> You shall stand before me.

> And if you bring forth the precious from the vile,
>> You shall be as my mouth.
> They shall turn unto you,
>> But you shall not turn unto them.

In the light of this passage and the experiences referred to, we may see the appropriateness of S. H. Blank's description of the prophet as "a man whose organ of speech was thought to be at the disposal of deity. Through the mouth of the prophet, God might announce his will and purpose—might become articulate."[8]

The prophet was the medium by which the word of God was given to men. In many instances the word is thought of as having independent existence, as if it were something physical and not simply the utterance of the prophet. For example, we read in Hos. 6:5:

> I [Yahweh] will hew them by the prophets;
> I will slay them by the words of my mouth.

In Isa. 9:8 the prophet says:

> A word has the Lord sent unto Jacob,
> And it will fall upon Israel.

Again, Second Isaiah compares the word of God to the rain or the snow which falls upon the earth, watering it and making plants grow, and says:

> So shall my word be that goes forth from my mouth:
> It shall not return unto me empty
> Except it do my pleasure
> And accomplish the purpose for which I sent it. (Isa. 55:11.)

In Jer. 23:29 we read:

> Is not my word like fire (says the Lord),
> And like a hammer that smashes rock?

---

[8] *Hebrew Union College Annual*, XV (1940), 21-22.

With such an understanding of the nature and importance of the word of God, a prophet could describe as the worst punishment upon a people the sending of famine—famine not for bread, but "for hearing the word of the Lord" (Amos. 8:11).

In the third place, it is clear that, although the prophet might know in advance that his message would be unfavorably received, he was not thereby deterred from giving it. This is most evident in the calls of Isaiah and Ezekiel, but it may have been involved in the experiences of all the prophets. Certainly not one of them could have felt, throughout his career and upon its conclusion, that he was a success in the popular sense. None of them were really heeded in their own day. Each may have had a few disciples who preserved the master's words, but every prophet gave messages which fell mostly upon deaf ears. Yet they were not disillusioned, and probably not greatly concerned over the reception they were accorded. They were not prophesying for the sake of the immediate results they might achieve; they did not care for pragmatic measurements. They prophesied because they had to, because they were under divine compulsion and could do no other.

Again, we may say that the effectiveness of a prophet—in the sight of the Deity, if not in the sight of men—was in no way determined by his own outward willingness. Isaiah is represented as volunteering to go for the Lord, but Jeremiah shrank from the prophetic mission. Yet no one could conclude that Isaiah was a truer prophet than Jeremiah. Whether a man volunteered or prophesied grudgingly, the important fact was that he accepted the burden placed upon him and performed the task to which he was assigned.

Finally, this discussion of the nature of the prophet's commission and task supports a recent explanation of the origin of the Hebrew word for prophet—*nābî*'. Scholars have long debated the etymology of this word. Some have suggested that it is derived from a verb meaning "to bubble up" or "to pour forth." While this might accurately describe the ecstatic prophet who spoke under abnormal emotion, it is hardly applicable to the great prophets; and, besides, one consonant in this verb is not correct. Others have suggested that the word is derived from a root meaning "to announce" or "to speak." While the prophet was undoubtedly a spokesman for God, the Hebrew word is passive rather than active in meaning. Recently William F. Albright has connected the word with an Akkadian verb meaning "to call" and so explains the Hebrew *nābī'* as meaning literally "one who is called (by God), one who has a vocation (from God)." [9] This is sound linguistically and is undeniably in accord with the prophets' own understanding of their nature and mission.

[9] *From the Stone Age to Christianity* (Baltimore: Johns Hopkins Press, 1940) pp. 231-32.

CHAPTER IV

THE PROPHETIC CRITICISM OF LIFE

IT HAS BECOME A COMMONPLACE OF THE MODERN VIEW OF THE OLD Testament that the prophets were not simply foretellers of the future —especially not of a far-distant future—but were primarily preachers of the will of God to the people of their own time. Prediction was indeed an important element in their work, perhaps more important than modern scholars generally admit. Nevertheless, the main concern of the prophets was not with a remote future but with their own day and their contemporaries.

The prophets were critics of the life of their own time. A critic is one who is able to judge, to express opinions concerning values, because he knows standards. A good critic does not always condemn. No judge finds guilty every criminal who comes to the bar; if he does so, he does not remain in office long. The prophets were able to pass criticism on the men and society of their day because they spoke in the name of a God who is a judge over men and their actions, not a patron of whatever the *status quo* happens to be. If the prophets seem usually to have passed adverse criticism and to have foretold only doom, it is because in the sight of God there was so much in men and society that failed to measure up to his high standards and needed to be rooted out or changed.

William Temple, the late Archbishop of Canterbury, said: "It is a great mistake to suppose that God is only, or even chiefly, concerned with religion."[1] He meant that God is not chiefly concerned with what *we* commonly mean by "religion"—going to church, making our offerings, praying, observing holidays, and the like. The prophets had a much broader view of what constitutes religion. The same author said: "The principles of conduct in all departments of life belong to the sphere of religion; for God is

[1] *The Hope of a New World* (New York: Macmillan, 1940), p. 70.

supreme over all life and at all points we must obey Him if we have faith in Him."[2] The point of emphasis in prophetic religion is the little word "all": *all* men should bring *all* of their lives under the whole will of God. The prophets did not recognize the distinction which we commonly make between the secular and the sacred. Men and society should consecrate to the will of God all their attitudes and all their actions.

In exercising the prophetic right of criticism according to divine standards, the prophets found many attitudes and actions of their contemporaries deserving of condemnation. The more important of these may be summarized under four headings: narrowness of vision, false leadership, abuse of economic power, and pride. These were the major sins in the eyes of the prophets.

NARROWNESS OF VISION

The Israelites of Amos' time must have been jolted out of their complacency when they heard that prophet cry out:

> Are you not unto me as the Ethiopians,
> O children of Israel?
> Did not I lead Israel
> From the land of Egypt,
> And the Philistines from Caphtor,
> And the Syrians from Kir? (9:7.)

Amos' fellow men had much to make them proud. They *did* have a better religion than surrounding nations. They *had* been given a revelation not vouchsafed to other peoples. Besides, they were prosperous economically, and at peace. But the Israelites accepted these things in a narrow and selfish spirit, believing that their God cared only for them and their destiny. Yahweh had made a covenant with them, and most Israelites believed the bond thus forged could not be severed. Amos asserted that their God, Yahweh, cared also—not

[2] *Ibid.,* p. 36.

as much perhaps (3:2), but *also*—for the black-skinned Ethiopians of Africa, and that he had controlled the exodus not only of Israel from Egypt but also of the hated Philistines from Caphtor (Crete and the near-by Aegean region), and of the Syrians from Kir (not definitely identified). Undoubtedly this was considered heresy by the Israelites and was one of the reasons for the expulsion of Amos from Bethel. A similar opinion of the sphere of Yahweh's activity is expressed in the oracles of Amos 1:3–2:3, in which the prophet proclaims Yahweh's coming punishment of Damascus, Gaza, Tyre, Edom, and other cities and peoples. Amos believed that Yahweh made ethical demands upon foreign nations, demands not as high as those made upon Israel but requiring at least the decent and humane treatment of enemies in time of war. He believed that Yahweh could punish foreign nations as well as Israel. Amos' hearers would have rejoiced in the proclamation of punishment upon these peoples, but they did not wish to accept the prophet's corollary that Yahweh was therefore their God, with a care and concern for their fate as well as for Israel's.

Isaiah, who had a long public career and was in close touch with the political scene, had to struggle against narrow nationalism. He tried to convince the Israelites and their leaders that Yahweh could use even foreign kings to accomplish his purposes. In a bold passage he speaks fervently of the Assyrian king—doubtless Sennacherib—as the rod of God's anger and the staff of his fury, sent against a godless nation as punishment for its sins (10:5 ff.). But the Assyrian king, says the prophet, must not suppose that he is accomplishing his victory over Israel by his own might and so become proud; if he becomes proud and arrogant, then Yahweh will destroy him too. The ax must not boast itself over the man who swings it, nor the saw magnify itself above him who uses it! Isaiah had indeed a large vision of the extent of God's power and purposes.

Many passages in the book of Isaiah suggest, however, that on one point Isaiah retained, or was converted to, a narrowness of view and taught that, whatever might happen to Judah in general, the capital city of Jerusalem would be spared. This doctrine of the "inviolability of Zion" seems to be stated in Isa. 31:5; 33:5-6; 37:33-35, and other verses. It is doubtful, however, that at any time Isaiah became a nationalist and led the Judaeans to believe that their capital city would be preserved regardless of their own attitudes and conduct. His true attitude toward Jerusalem, especially in the crisis of 701 B.C., when Sennacherib invaded Palestine, is expressed by passages such as 22:1-14 and 29:1-4.

The former of these, 22:1-14, must have been uttered during the siege of the city, or just after Hezekiah's surrender to Sennacherib. The prophet bitterly condemns the people for their revelry and feasting at a time when they ought to be sorrowful. God, he says, has called them to weeping and wailing and humility, but they are feasting and drinking and making the most of the present with the feeling that "tomorrow we die." They have looked to military measures and armament rather than to God. Surely Isaiah could not promise the salvation of Jerusalem to such people with such conduct!

Even stronger is the condemnation by Isaiah in 29:1-4. This is a "woe" uttered against "Ariel," a name for Jerusalem used—in this instance, at least—because of its association with the name of the underworld, like *Aralu* in Babylonian. Isaiah ironically bids the people continue their festivals, but promises that God will bring distress upon Ariel, making it indeed like the underworld. In verse 3 he says in the name of Yahweh:

> I shall encamp against you, like David,
> And hem you in with siegeworks,
> And raise up ramparts against you!

In the light of passages such as these, we can hardly believe that Isaiah taught the impregnability of Jerusalem because of its protection by Yahweh. We know well, both from Sennacherib's own annals [3] and from II Kings 18:13-21, that Sennacherib sent an army against Judah which devastated much of the country and laid siege to Jerusalem. But Hezekiah, apparently after the desertion of some of his best troops, surrendered and offered tribute to the Assyrian king. As a result the siege was lifted and the city spared. Later editors of Isaiah's book—as well as historians of the nation—believed, probably in part on the basis of Isa. 28:16, that Isaiah had taught the inviolability of Zion; and so they edited his book to make him teach such an idea. But it is impossible to believe that the prophet who was so great an internationalist and taught such a complete trust in God was less courageous than his contemporary Micah and his successor Jeremiah, both of whom predicted the possible destruction of Jerusalem and the temple.[4]

In the seventh century Jeremiah contended against narrow men who believed that they were protected by a nationalistic deity. Their attitude was somewhat promoted by the Deuteronomic reformation, which came in the reign of Josiah (621 B.C.). This reformation had many admirable features, such as the purification of worship and the establishment of greater social justice. But it intensified nationalism both in religion and in politics. Josiah succeeded in freeing himself from Assyrian domination and influences in religion. But the centralization of sacrificial worship in the capital city served also to centralize political control there and to enhance the power of the king, and the Deuteronomic reformation actually promoted greater nationalism. An especially bitter attitude is expressed in Deuteronomy toward the Ammonites and Moabites (23:3-6).

Jeremiah opposed materialistic dependence on the temple in Jerusalem and the narrow view that Yahweh must protect the nation as long as the temple stood. In a sermon which caused his arrest (chaps. 7, 26) Jeremiah predicted that unless the people experienced

[3] See *Ancient Records of Assyria and Babylonia,* ed. D. D. Luckenbill (Chicago: University of Chicago Press, 1927), II, 119-21.

[4] My view of the events of 701 B.C. agrees largely with that of K. Fullerton, "Viewpoints in the Discussion of Isaiah's Hopes for the Future," *Journal of Biblical Literature,* XLI (1922), 1-101.

moral reformation the Jerusalem temple would be destroyed, just as the Shiloh temple had been devastated centuries earlier. Later, when the Judaean kingdom was invaded by the Chaldaean armies, Jeremiah preached that the God of the Jews was using the Chaldaeans as his instrument to punish them for their sins. As Isaiah had referred to Sennacherib as the rod of God's anger, Jeremiah could call Nebuchadrezzar, the Chaldaean king, the "servant" of Yahweh (27:6), who would serve him by accomplishing his purposes. Jeremiah must have seemed to his compatriots a traitor, a Jewish Quisling, for he counseled submission to Babylon even when the city of Jerusalem was under siege.

Subsequently, when Jerusalem fell and many of the Jews were exiled to Babylonia, Jeremiah again showed the largeness of his vision in a letter he wrote to the exiles. This remarkable document is preserved in chapter 29. In it the prophet advised the exiles to build houses, plant vineyards, marry and give in marriage, and in general to settle down and seek the welfare of the communities in which they were placed. He then told them that not even in Babylonia would they be divorced from their own God, for there he would hear them and be found of them if with all their heart they would seek him. Jeremiah believed that the true worship of the living God was not dependent on the Holy Land or the temple, but only on the pure heart. His depth and breadth of view were hardly shared by many in his day.

Of all the Old Testament prophets the one who demonstrated the widest vision was Second Isaiah. In him the ethical monotheism and universalism latent in the teaching of earlier prophets came to full fruition. Like Isaiah and Jeremiah, he believed that the God of the Hebrews could use a foreign king to do his bidding and help accomplish his purposes. With Second Isaiah this king was Cyrus the Persian, to whom he refers as the shepherd—that is, the ruler—of Yahweh (44:28), and even as "his anointed" (45:1). In ancient Israel kings and priests were anointed as representatives of God; so Cyrus is to represent God. Second Isaiah must have entertained great expectations from Cyrus—expectations that were only partly fulfilled. The vision of this prophet went beyond the restoration of Israel to her old land. He envisaged nothing short of the universal sway of Yahweh, when all men would recognize his sovereignty. Through the witness of the Suffering Servant the time would come when all would worship Yahweh:

> For to me every knee shall bow,
>   Every tongue shall swear, saying,
> "With Yahweh alone
>   Are righteousness and strength." (45:23-24.)

It is somewhat surprising that Second Isaiah betrays his own universalism in his attitude toward Egypt, Ethiopia, and Seba in 43:3 and 45:14, picturing them as becoming servants to Israel. There is no adequate reason to consider these verses as secondary; hence they must be regarded only as a lapse on the part of the prophet himself.

Jesus of Nazareth was like the ancient Hebrew prophet in his scorn of narrowness in attitude and vision. He lived at a time when universal, ethical monotheism was firmly established in Israel, at least in theory. But he saw many men who did not live according to their theory. His scorn was directed especially toward those Pharisees who narrowly believed that God's favor was restricted to their own group and to others who were able to follow their rules; and he refused to ally himself with the Zealots, a fanatical body of nationalists who ultimately led the Jews in the revolt against Rome in A.D. 66-70. While it may well be true, as several modern scholars —including Christians—have shown, that not all Pharisees of the first century were hypocritical and "pharisaical," and that some of the invectives against Pharisees in the gospels reflect the antagonism between the early Christian community and the Jews, there must have been many Pharisees, particularly of the strict Shammaite party, who merited Jesus' scorn. Certainly the practices of many betrayed the high ideals they professed. Jesus would not tolerate a narrowness of vision which was a practical denial of the sovereignty and goodness of God.

FALSE LEADERSHIP

The government of the Hebrew people was loosely organized, and their society was usually an uneasy balance between the old nomadic society of the desert and the Canaanite culture of Palestine. Among the nomads, ideals of brotherhood and equality were dominant, and men who were full members of a tribe were considered equal. Leaders achieved their positions more by age and ability than anything else, and were considered as "first among equals." Canaanite society, on the other hand, was feudalistic, and ideals of aristocracy rather than of democracy prevailed.

The leaders of the Israelites were of two groups, civil and religious. The civil leaders were the king and various officials, generally designated as princes and elders. The king was not only the chief administrator but also chief justice, first soldier, and chief priest—in theory, if not always in practice. The princes and elders performed numerous administrative and judicial functions not clearly defined in every case. The religious leaders were the priests and prophets. Priests not only offered sacrifices and performed various religious rites but also had a prominent role in the formation and administration of law. There were undoubtedly a very large number of prophets, many more than we are accustomed to think from the paucity of writing prophets. Some of them were retainers at court who consulted the oracles on important occasions, and others were cultic prophets attached to sanctuaries.

We divide these leaders into two groups only for the sake of convenience. In practice they were closely associated. In ancient Israel, church and state were not separate; in fact, those two terms would hardly be recognized by an ancient Hebrew. Religion was one of the principal bulwarks of the state, and the state in turn patronized religion.

The prophets did not hesitate to condemn any of the leaders, from the king down to the humblest official, secular or religious. As

Nathan had rebuked David in earlier times for his sin of murder and adultery, and Elijah had condemned Ahab for the murder of Naboth and expropriation of his property, so the great prophets condemned whatever seemed to them wrong in the activities or policies of the kings and his princes. Isaiah and Jeremiah were at times consulted by the kings in important crises. The prophets did not then shrink from pronouncing judgments which they knew would be unwelcome and unheeded.

Isaiah complains that "the leaders of this people have become misleaders; those who are led are swallowed up" (9:16; cf. 3:12). Chapter 28 presents a vivid account of a contest between Isaiah and the priests and prophets (vss. 7-19). He accuses the religious leaders of being intoxicated with strong drink. They in turn say that he only speaks "baby talk," and give an imitation of it in monosyllables. The prophet thereupon announces that they will be destroyed in the coming destruction by a foreign ruler.

No prophet was more bitter and outspoken in his denunciation of false leadership than Micah. He excoriated all groups, and specified the nature of their sins, as the following excerpts (3:1-2, 5-6, 11) show:

> Hear now, you heads of Jacob,
>   And rulers of the house of Israel:
> Is it not your task to know justice,
>   You who hate good and love evil,
> Who snatch their skin from upon them,
>   And their flesh from upon their bones?
>
> .   .   .   .
>
> Thus says Yahweh concerning the prophets,
>   The misleaders of my people,
> Who when they are well fed
>   Pronounce "Peace!"
> But declare war against him
>   Who pays not well:
> Therefore, you shall have night without vision,
>   And darkness without divination;

> The sun shall set upon the prophets,
>   And the day shall become dark upon them.
>
> . . . .
>
> Her [Jerusalem's] chiefs judge for a bribe,
>   Her priests give oracles for hire,
> And her prophets divine for money,
>   And yet they lean upon the Lord, saying,
> "Is not the Lord in our midst?
>   Evil cannot overtake us!"

Hosea complained that it had become "like people, like priest" (4:9). The priests were apparently no better than the people, and so were not really giving leadership at all. In similar mood Jeremiah asserted (5:30-31) that the religious leaders were venal, and the masses did not want them otherwise:

> An astonishing and horrible thing
>   Has occurred in the land:
> The prophets prophesy lies,
>   The priests scrape into their own hands,
> And my people love it so!
>   So what will you do in the end?

Ezekiel had very bitter words for the false prophets. He called them "jackals among ruins" who had neither "gone up into the breaches nor built up a wall for the house of Israel" (13:4-5). In chapter 34 he condemned the rulers as false "shepherds" who had not looked after the safety and welfare of their flocks but had sought only to satisfy their own desires.

Many similar passages could be quoted or referred to, but these well illustrate the boldness of the prophets in condemning those false leaders who betrayed the trust placed in them by their God and his people. The basis of the prophetic condemnation was that these leaders had not accepted their positions as a trust but rather had used them for selfish gain. As a result, they had not only failed to furnish the leadership which their group needed but had even become "misleaders"—a word used above to translate a Hebrew expression meaning literally "those who cause to err." Thus civil rulers had tried to lead to national honor and glory upon paths of military success and material prosperity, not counting the cost in human life and misery which these entailed. They had been encouraged by the prophets of weal who, for the sake of popularity and money, had predicted success, putting forth their own ideas for the "word of the Lord."

Jesus lived in a time when the Jewish nation was not politically independent but under Roman rule. He apparently acquiesced in the Roman government, not encouraging revolt but declaring that the Jews should "render to Caesar those things that belong to Caesar, and to God those that belong to God" (Mark 12:17). He did not hesitate, however, to condemn as roundly as had the Old Testament prophets the religious misleaders of his day. He spoke of the Pharisees as "blind guides," who placed burdens upon others which they themselves refused to bear, and who were over-meticulous about unimportant religious dues but careless of "the weightier matters of the law—justice, mercy, and faith" (Matt. 23:23). The Sadducean priesthood likewise had failed in its positions of trust, and Jesus found it necessary to cleanse the temple of the corruptions which they had allowed to creep into it for money's sake. If Jesus did not find occasion to excoriate the Roman rulers of Palestine, he did not shrink any more than his predecessors from excoriating those Jewish leaders whose guidance in matters both religious and secular was lacking in a sense of responsibility and stewardship.

Abuse of Economic Power

Abuse of economic power was a third evil condemned by most of the prophets. This is, of course, closely related to the sin just discussed, for any position of leadership involves power. And power is always potentially corrupting to its possessor. Economic power and its abuse should, however, be discussed separately, for the Hebrew prophets were especially sensitive to this evil and some of them devoted much space to it. They knew that the fascination of material-ism and of economic power exerts a strongly corrupting influence on men.

By the middle of the eighth century an economic situation had risen which is clearly reflected in the book of Amos and in the work of other prophets of that and the succeeding century. In Amos' day Israel was prosperous and at peace. There were a few wealthy fami-lies who lived in large, fine houses filled with ivory-inlaid furniture. They ate rich food and spent much of their leisure time in banquet-ing. The wives were idle and urged their husbands on in oppression. On the other hand, there was a large mass of very poor people who were frequently exploited by the wealthy and seldom found justice in the law courts.

How did this situation arise? It seems a far cry from the desert democracy and the principles of fraternity and equality which we associate with the earliest stage of Hebrew life. We cannot trace in every detail the process by which this social cleavage arose, but we can be sure of some of its broad outlines.

As in the social organization, there was an important difference in ideal between the Canaanite and the Hebrew system of economics. This can best be seen in their respective attitudes toward land. Among the Hebrews land was not a simple commodity to be bought and sold on the open market. The land was really the Lord's, they believed, and he had given it in trust to families and clans. Theo-retically, land could be transferred only when an insolvent debtor had to turn it over to his creditors, or when a thief had to pay a fine. In the former case, the law of redemption provided that a near relative should have the duty and privilege of buying back the land at the earliest opportunity, in order that the bond between the family and its land might not be permanently broken (Lev. 25). These ideals about land were due in part to the desert heritage of the Hebrews and in part to the early influence of the Hurrians—called

Horites in the Old Testament—among whom the principle of the inalienability of real property was very strong.[5]

Canaanite society, on the other hand, was feudalistic, as we have already seen. Land was apparently concentrated in the hands of the aristocracy, and was considered a commodity to be bought and sold on the market. Some of the differences between Hebrew and Canaanite ideals may be seen in the story of Naboth's vineyard (I Kings 21). The Hebrew king Ahab desired the vineyard of a small landowner, and offered either to give him another parcel of ground in exchange or to buy the plot. Naboth refused to part with his ancestral inheritance. Ahab was ready to admit defeat, however reluctantly, when Jezebel stepped in to get the vineyard for her husband. She arranged matters so that Naboth was put to death, and then the king expropriated his property. Jezebel was a Phoenician princess—that is, a Canaanite—with ideals regarding land and a king's prerogatives which differed from those of Ahab.

By the middle of the eighth century there had arisen a class of wealthy landowners among the Hebrews. They had, in the words of Isaiah, joined house to house and added field to field (5:8) until much of the land was in the hands of a few and many peasants were deprived of their property and compelled to become day laborers or slaves. It may well be that the procedures followed by the grasping wealthy were usually legal; they probably lent money at high rates of interest with land as security and then foreclosed on the mortgages when the debtors were unable to pay. We do not know what the interest rates were in eighth-century Israel. In the Assyrian empire of that time, interest was usually 20 per cent or higher.[6] In the sixth century the Jews of Elephantine in Egypt were

[5] Most of our information regarding the Hurrians comes from the cuneiform tablets discovered at Nuzu in northeastern Iraq. For a brief summary see C. H. Gordon, "Biblical Customs and the Nuzu Tablets," *The Biblical Archaeologist*, III (1940), 1-12.

[6] See Morris Jastrow, *The Civilization of Babylonia and Assyria* (Philadelphia, Lippincott, 1915), p. 340.

charged 60 per cent.[7] In Palestine the rates were probably higher than in Assyria, for the country was poorer, but perhaps not as high as Elephantine, where the Jews were living as foreigners. It is not difficult to see that droughts and other causes of famine, military invasion, plague, and the like took a heavy toll of the small peasants, who when unable to pay their creditors had to go into slavery or become laborers, whose lot was little better than that of slaves. We should not be surprised that Deuteronomy forbade the charging of interest to fellow Hebrews (23:19), although the law may have been largely paper law only.

In addition to these conditions which produced a small class of landed aristocracy and a large mass of landless laborers and slaves, we must suppose that other conditions accounted for the rise of a wealthy merchant class. It was Solomon who set the Hebrews upon the road to being international merchants. He exploited the natural resources in copper and iron of the region south of the Dead Sea, exporting ingots and manufactured objects in return for products his country lacked. He established an extensive trade in horses and chariots, as is stated in I Kings 10:26-28 and as archaeologists have verified at Megiddo and elsewhere. He had a fleet of merchant ships based at Ezion-Geber. Solomon was thus a great patron of commerce and industry.[8]

In the years between Solomon and Amos, international and domestic commerce must have grown. When Amos prophesied, the merchants were most avid in their pursuit of wealth, not hesitating to be dishonest if they thought it necessary. They were restless on the Sabbaths and other holy days when they could not trade; they gave small measures and charged inflated prices; they sold the refuse of grain; thus they trampled upon the needy and sought to stamp out the poor (Amos 8:4-6). Many a man may well have been at once a large landowner and a prosperous merchant, although of course not

[7] See *Aramaic Papyri of the Fifth Century B.C.*, ed. Arthur E. Cowley (Oxford, 1923), pp. 29, 33.

[8] For archaeological discoveries bearing on the reign of Solomon, see my article "Solomon in All His Glory," *Journal of Bible and Religion*, VIII (1940), 27-30.

all merchants became wealthy. The rich merchants and landowners were favored by civil administrators, including judges, whom they were able to bribe. In any case, the poor were exploited and made poorer while a few piled up more riches than they could use.

In general the prophets were advocates of the dispossessed and exploited poor, crying out against injustices perpetrated by the wealthy. Amos and Micah are especially bitter in their denunciation of the abuse of economic power. It is probable that they were from the poor class themselves. Isaiah also denounced the wealthy, but he may have come from a somewhat higher social class, although this is not certain. He was more concerned than either Amos or Micah with the effects of injustice on the wealthy men themselves. Jeremiah did not inveigh against economic abuses as much as his predecessors, but he was by no means silent concerning them. It may be that by his time conditions were slightly improved, partly because of the Deuteronomic reforms. Jeremiah himself came from a family that owned land, as chapter 32 shows. Hosea had little to say about economic injustices, for he was concerned with other sins. Ezekiel and Second Isaiah likewise concerned themselves little with this subject, for in their day both rich and poor were imperiled by a foreign power. However, when Ezekiel portrayed his ethical ideals, as in chapters 18 and 34, he stood squarely for economic justice.

We have noted Amos' unusually vivid description of the economic evils of his time. His denunciation of those responsible for such evils was equally vivid. After describing the sins of surrounding nations (1:3–2:3), he set forth the transgressions of Israel:

> They have sold the righteous for silver,
>   And the needy for a pair of sandals—
> They who trample upon the heads of the poor,
>   And thrust aside the humble in the way. (2:6-7.)

After depicting the evils of the merchants (8:4-6), Amos declared that Yahweh had sworn by the pride of Jacob, "I will never forget all their doings!"

Micah, who came from Moresheth-Gath, a village in the Shephelah of southwestern Palestine, represented the peasantry. He denounced the rapacious wealthy with a vigor that may well have come from having suffered unfortunate experiences at their hands:

> Woe to those who devise iniquity
>   And work out evil on their beds;
> Early in the morning they carry it out,
>   For it is in their power.
> They covet fields and seize them,
>   And houses, and snatch them up.
> They crush a man and his house,
>   A man and his inheritance. (2:1-2.)

> The women of my people you dispossess
>   From their pleasant homes,
> And from their children you take away
>   My glory forever. (2:9.)

The oracle of Isaiah in which he shows concern for the effect of economic injustice upon the wealthy people themselves is 5:8-10:

> Woe to those who join house to house,
>   And add field to field,
> Till there is no more room,
>   And you are left dwelling alone in the land!
> Therefore the Lord of hosts has sworn in my ears:
> "Verily many houses shall become a desolation,
>   Great and fine, without inhabitant.
> For ten acres of vineyard shall yield but a bath,
>   And a homer of seed shall yield but an ephah."

This is a condemnation in which the punishment fits the crime. The wealthy who sought more and more isolation are promised that they shall have complete isolation, without the poor to sustain them; and their lands eventually are to be so worked out as to become unproductive.

In another passage (3:14-15) Isaiah revealed one of the strongest reasons for the prophetic denunciation of the oppression practiced by the wealthy: it did violence to the prophetic ideal that all the Israelites should constitute the people of Yahweh—"my people":

> The Lord will come in judgment
>   On the elders and princes of his people:
> "It is you that have ravaged the vineyard;
>   The plunder of the poor is in *your* houses.
> What mean you that you crush my people,
>   And grind the face of the poor?"

In similar vein he pronounces woe upon those who "snatch away the justice due the poor of my people" (10:2).

Jeremiah does not have many passages dealing with economic injustice, but that such injustice was still rampant in his day and that his attitude did not differ from that of other prophets is shown by a passage such as 5:27-29:

> As a cage is full of birds,
>   So their houses are full of deceit;
> Thus they grow great and rich,
>   They become fat and sleek.
> They transgress my words for evil,
>   They plead not a cause—
> The cause of the orphan, that they may succeed,
>   And the right of the needy they do not defend.
> For such things shall I not punish them?
>   Says the Lord.
> Upon such a people
>   Shall not my soul take vengeance?

Jeremiah pronounced condemnation against King Jehoiakim because he built his palace by unrighteousness and injustice, using his neighbor's labor without wages (22:13). In 17:11 an amusing, but rather profound, figure is used to describe the fate of a wealthy man who gets his riches by injustice:

> Like a partridge hatching eggs she has not laid,
> Is one who amasses wealth by injustice:
> In the middle of his days he must leave it,
> And at the end he will be a fool.

When we turn from the Old Testament prophets to Jesus, we find that he had a great deal to say regarding wealth and its use or abuse. There can be no question that he was much concerned with economic subjects, for he often spoke of them. One immediately recalls certain well-known words: "Lay not up for yourselves treasures on the earth" (Matt. 6:19). "It is easier for a camel to pass through the eye of a needle than for a rich man to enter the kingdom of God" (Matt. 19:24). "You cannot serve God and mammon" (Luke 16:13). Or one recalls outstanding parables in which wealth and poverty play an important part, such as that about the rich man and Lazarus (Luke 16:19-31). Or one may remember the story of the rich young ruler who could not enter the Kingdom because he would not renounce his wealth (Mark 10:17 ff.).

The Gospel of Luke gives a particularly large number of incidents and teachings which deal with economic matters. In Luke's version of the Beatitudes, Jesus seems to bless those who are materially poor and pronounce woe upon those who are wealthy in material goods:

> Blessed are you poor, for yours is the kingdom of God!
> Blessed are you that hunger now, for you shall be filled!
>
> .   .   .   .
> But woe unto you that are rich, for you have received your consolation!
> Woe unto you that are full now, for you shall hunger!
>
> (6:20-21, 24-25.)

The teachings of Jesus regarding wealth and economic power have been the subject of numerous discussions from his own day to the present. Some have made of Jesus a patron of poverty. Others have pictured him as the leader of a proletarian revolution, as Bouck White did in *The Call of the Carpenter*. Still others have tried to tone down or explain away his teachings on wealth. The words of

Jesus have been used to buttress a capitalistic system as well as to prove that a socialistic or communistic system is ideal.

We must remember that Jesus came from a poor family, Joseph being a carpenter. His was not a poverty-stricken home, but it certainly was not one of wealth, and Jesus had to work with his hands. He could speak to the poor as one of their own, and most of his followers doubtless were from the poorer classes, although some of them were rich, like Zacchaeus.

It seems that Jesus' primary concern was not with the social effects of wealth but with the moral effects on the individual of the pursuit and possession of wealth. In this respect he differed largely from the Old Testament prophets; they lived in days when there was little individualism and the sense of social solidarity was very strong. Although not wholly unmindful of the effects of wealth on its possessors, they were more concerned with what the concentration of wealth in a few hands did for the whole people of the Lord, keeping them from being *my people*. Jesus may have condemned the wealthy for exploiting the poor; whether he did or not depends largely upon whether Luke accurately reports Jesus' teachings or colors them with his own attitude toward economic questions. At any rate, the carpenter of Nazareth was concerned primarily with what the pursuit and possession of wealth does to a man, dividing his loyalty, making him proud and covetous, separating him from both God and his fellow men. He wanted men to give undivided allegiance to God and his kingdom. Wealth and everything else which might hinder such allegiance must be renounced. Jesus wanted men to learn to place first values first. He knew "the deceitfulness of riches" (Matt. 13:22).

Perhaps these two sayings best summarize Jesus' attitude: "A man's life consists not in having more possessions than he needs"; [9] and "You cannot serve God and Mammon."

[9] This is Charles F. Kent's translation of a difficult verse, Luke 12:15, in *The Social Teachings of the Prophets and Jesus* (New York: Scribner, 1917), p. 226.

PRIDE

A fourth sin which the prophets condemned with all their power was pride. Of course pride is an important ingredient of the three evils already considered. Narrowness of vision rises partly from false national and class pride. Betrayal of trust by leaders comes from pride in position and failure to interpret leadership in unselfish terms. Abuse of economic power is often based upon a sinful pride in one's economic accomplishments and overweening trust in material goods and economic power. But to many of the prophets, as well as to other Old Testament writers, pride was the basic sin, involving trust in man and his works rather than in the power and goodness of God. Also, this sin led to other evils in addition to the ones we have already noted, especially to self-satisfied and parasitic living and to dependence on military power and other material things rather than on spiritual resources.

Isaiah is the Old Testament prophet most noted for his denunciation of pride. Emphasizing above all the necessity for man to trust and have faith in the God of holiness and majesty, he could not but view pride as the worst of all sins, for it is denial of the trustworthiness and might of God. Perhaps the strongest passage in his book is the following (2:12-17), in which everything that is proud in nature and in man is the object of God's destruction:

> For the Lord of hosts has a day
> Against all that is proud and high,
>   And against all that is lofty and tall:
> Against all cedars of Lebanon,
>   And against all oaks of Bashan;
> Against all lofty mountains,
>   And against all high hills;
> Against every high tower,
>   And against every fortified wall;
> Against all refinery ships,[10]

[10] For this translation of the Hebrew 'aniyyōth tarshīsh, cf. William F. Albright, *Bulletin of the American Schools of Oriental Research*, No. 83 (October 1941), pp. 21-22.

> And against all pleasure boats.
> The haughtiness of man will be humbled,
>   And the loftiness of man will be brought low,
> And the Lord alone will be exalted
>   On that day!

The linking together in this passage of various things in nature and the works of man with man's own pride may be taken partly as figurative language, but it also shows that the prophet had a strong sense of the bond existing between man and nature. There are other passages in the prophets that evidence the same attitude.[11]

Isaiah frequently spoke elsewhere of pride and its works. He pronounced woe upon those who were "wise in their own eyes" (5: 21). He denounced those Samaritans who

> In the pride and haughtiness of their heart said,
>   "Bricks have fallen, but with hewn stone we shall rebuild;
> Sycamores have been cut down, but with cedars we shall replace them."
>   (9:9b-10.)

In the passage dealing with Sennacherib, the Assyrian king, he pointed out that, after Yahweh had completed his punishment of Israel by the use of Assyria as a tool, he would then punish the latter nation for her proud belief that her military accomplishments had come through her own power (10:7-15). Isaiah disapproved of the alliances which the kings of his time made with Egypt, primarily because they expressed dependence upon "flesh" rather than upon "spirit"—that is, on man rather than God (30:1-5; 31:1-4). In 22: 1-14 he vividly portrayed the confidence of Judah in military measures rather than in God, and the stupidly callous revelry which accompanied this supremely false confidence.

Other Old Testament prophets condemned pride. Amos showed how the luxury and idleness of the rich had led to self-satisfied and self-confident living that ignored the true welfare of the nation:

[11] See below, pp. 158-59.

Woe to them who are at ease in Zion,
  And the self-confident in the mount of Samaria!

.   .   .   .

You who put far away the evil day,
  And bring near the year of violence.
They who lie on beds of ivory,
  And stretch out on divans,
Who eat lambs from the flock,
  And calves from the stall,
Who sing to the music of lyre,
  Composing songs for themselves, like David,
Who drink bowls of wine,
  And anoint themselves with finest oils,
But are not grieved over the affliction of Joseph—
Therefore, now, shall they be the first to go into exile,
  And the shout of the revelers shall die away! (6:1, 3-7.)

In similar vein was his prophecy against the women of Samaria, whom he called kine of Bashan—a region noted for its sleek, fat cattle—who lived parasitic lives, spending their time in idleness and drunkenness and goading their husbands into further exploitation of the poor. Isaiah likewise cast scorn upon the "daughters of Zion" because they "became haughty" and behaved with arrogance and self-display (3:16-4:1).

In a very interesting passage Jeremiah contrasts false boasting with a kind of boasting which may be considered legitimate: "Let not the wise man boast in his wisdom, nor the hero boast in his strength. Let not the rich man boast in his wealth. But let the man who must boast, boast in this, that he understands and knows me—that I am the Lord who practices fidelity, justice, and righteousness on the earth; for in such things do I delight." (9:23-24.)

Jesus of Nazareth stood in the prophetic succession in his view of pride. It may appear strange that the word "pride" occurs only once in the gospels (Mark 7:22). Jesus apparently said little directly about pride or about proud men as such. But it is abundantly certain that to him pride was a major sin, for it interfered with the one thing which Jesus demanded above all: repentance toward God and obedience to his will. Self-renunciation and the renunciation of all false objects of confidence were necessary to entrance into the Kingdom of God. The pride of the rich young ruler in his wealth kept him from the Kingdom. And so, in the view of Jesus, did pride in anything; for the demands of the Kingdom were for humility, obedience, and service.

WERE THE PROPHETS CHAMPIONS OF A CLASS?

We turn now to an important question that naturally rises: Were the prophets champions of a class, of the poor against the wealthy, of the exploited masses against their oppressors? The question does not permit of an unequivocal Yes or No answer. In some respects the prophets do appear as champions of the poor and oppressed; in others they are not class advocates at all.

Some of the prophets must have come from the poorer groups of society, especially Amos and Micah. Jesus, it appears, was from a relatively poor family—from the 'am hā-'āretz ("the people of the land") a designation of a group which included largely the poor but really comprehended all who did not have the learning or time or inclination to keep the laws as the Pharisees interpreted them. The followers of Jesus must have come largely from this group.

Most of the prophets clearly did express great sympathy for the downtrodden masses, and some spoke scathingly of the wealthy oppressors. They opposed all manner of exploitation, economic as well as religious. They must have felt that the poor particularly needed defense, the defense of the Lord, because they had not the social nor economic power with which to defend themselves.

These facts must not be denied, but it would nevertheless be incorrect to conclude that the prophets were merely champions of the poor, or that they were advocates of the class struggle after the manner of the modern Marxist. They did not desire simply the abolition of wealth and the wealthy classes. They desired the correction of abuses in the distribution of wealth, but above all they denounced sin in all classes wherever it manifested itself. This can be seen from a number of specific prophetic passages.

In Isa. 5:8-24 the prophet pronounces woe upon several groups. The first is the land monopolists, but he proceeds to denounce drunken revelers, brazen sinners, those who deny moral distinctions, the conceited, and others. We surely cannot suppose that all the sins here condemned were committed only by the wealthy! The prophet uses, in verse 13 and in verse 14, words which may be translated "nobility" and "masses," and both classes are described as suffering punishment. In Jer. 5 the prophet reports a search for honesty and justice among the people of Jerusalem, but admits that he finds them neither among the "poor ones" (vs. 4) nor the "great ones" (vs. 5). In verses 30-31 he describes a condition in which prophets and priests are false and "my people" love to have them so! Ezek. 22: 23-29 catalogues the offenses of several groups enumerated as rulers, priests, princes, prophets, and, finally, the common people—'am hā-'āretz.

Far from merely championing the cause of a class, the prophets criticized all classes, denouncing sin wherever it appeared, because they wanted all classes to unite in being *one* people under God. The prophetic attitude is well summed up in the saying of Jesus: "Except you repent, you shall *all* likewise perish!" (Luke 13:3, 5.)

Were the Prophets Social Reformers?

Another important question which arises is this: Were the prophets social reformers? This question likewise does not admit of a simple answer. It is complicated by the further question whether the prophets expected society as they knew it to continue, or whether they looked to a divine intervention in the near future to destroy the land, or at least the evil in the land.

Full consideration of this question is given in chapter VI, where we shall see that the prophets varied among themselves in their view of the future, the earlier prophets being more definitely predictors of doom than the later ones, who held out hope for the continuation of life and society more or less as they had been known. Nevertheless, all the prophets made moral demands in the name of their God upon the people to whom they preached, and these moral demands had important implications for social reform.

There is no denying that the prophets were generally more concerned with society as a whole, and with social systems and institutions, than with the individual. It is almost an axiom of modern interpretation of the Old Testament that there was little or no individualism among the Hebrews until the time of Ezekiel. It may be false to make an absolute distinction between individualism and the principle of social solidarity, but the prophets had in view mainly the whole social group, the nation, rather than the individual Israelite. The individualism which is ultimately found in Ezekiel (14:12-20; 18; 33:10-20) is exaggerated and somewhat unrealistic.

The prophets did not, however, have any blueprints for the ideal social system, nor did they attempt to change social institutions. They did tend to idealize the Mosaic period, but it was the spiritual and religious ideals of that time which they wished to recover, not the specific social conditions which then prevailed. They did not agree with the Rechabites, a group who refused to live in houses, to till the soil, or to drink wine, all of which symbolized to them the corruptions of agrarian society. The Rechabites were sociological primitivists who wished to revive or continue the exact social conditions of the nomadic life. The prophets do not appear to have sought to do this, although Jeremiah did praise the Rechabites for their fidelity and loyalty to their principles (chap. 35).

The prophets, then, were not social reformers in detail. They were concerned, however, to insist that social systems, institutions, and practices be judged by their consequences for *all* the people, and not for a favored few. They opposed all reliance on vested interests. They would have agreed that social institutions must serve man; as Jesus said, "The Sabbath was made for man, and not man for the Sabbath" (Mark 2:27). Social systems must conform to God's requirements of justice, kindness, and humility. This was the basic attitude of the Old Testament prophets and of Jesus.

The prophets were not economists or political scientists. But they did deal with questions of fundamental importance for all who are interested in social systems, and they furnish the controlling principles by which both society and the individual are to be judged.

CHAPTER V

THE PROPHETIC VIEW OF HISTORY: THE PAST

THE HEBREWS WERE THE FIRST PEOPLE IN THE ANCIENT WORLD TO HAVE a sense of history. They were thus the first to conceive of God as a God of history, manifesting himself on the stage of time and controlling the destiny of men and nations. The Hebrews affirmed the reality and importance of time. To them it was not an illusion, something from which man must escape, but something which must be redeemed.

It is characteristic of the Hebrews that one of their number—or a group—wrote the first history of the world four or five centuries before Herodotus, the falsely reputed "Father of History." The failure to recognize this fact is due in part to prejudice of secular historians today toward the Bible and the ignorance of many concerning pre-Greek civilization.

This first historian was a man known to Old Testament students as "The Yahwist," or simply by the symbol J. He is usually dated about 850 B.C.; but it is more probable that he lived a century earlier, during the reign of Solomon, who was a patron of literature as well as of architecture, industry, and international commerce.[1] The work of J is now contained within the Pentateuch and the books of Joshua, Judges, and Samuel, constituting the earliest strand of historical narrative in those books. The Yahwist wrote universal history which culminated in the history of his own nation. He began with the creation of the world, told the myths of the primordial beginnings, described the adventures and promises of the patriarchs, recorded the epic events of the exodus from Egypt and the conquest of the

[1] The dating of J in the reign of Solomon is more certain if, as we have supposed, the narrative known to scholars as the "early source" in Samuel is a continuation of the Yahwistic narrative of the Pentateuch and Joshua-Judges. This seems probable, but has never been proved in detail. See Robert H. Pfeiffer, *Introduction to the Old Testament* (New York: Harper, 1941), p. 341.

Promised Land, described the establishment of the monarchy, and ended with the reign of David. He relied in part upon oral tradition, but he may have had written sources as well. He was indeed a collector of traditions, sometimes recording divergent traditions without attempting to reconcile them.

The work of J was more epic in scope, of finer literary merit, and dominated by greater unity of purpose than the work of Herodotus. The fact that he was not as self-conscious a writer of history, and did not state his purpose and methods as clearly as the Greek writer, does not make him less successful. A modern scholar has said: "Judged by results then, rather than by profession, the Hebrew historians reached at least as great success in the investigation and intelligent explanation of facts as Herodotus, and did this at an earlier date."[2]

THE MEANING OF THE WORD "HISTORY"

When we use the word "history" we may mean either events happening in time, or the record of those events. In the former sense, everything that has ever occurred either in nature or in human life is a part of history, but no human mind can ever record or comprehend even a small fraction of that total. Nor is it important that one should. Much of history in this sense is trivial and worthy only of oblivion.

History in the second sense may be either objective or subjective. Objective history is a mere narration of events as they have occurred, with no interpretation of their meaning. In spite of the pretensions of the modern historian, absolutely objective history is extremely rare, if not wholly impossible of attainment, and it is actually of little value and less interest. Subjective history seeks not simply to recover what actually occurred but to explain why it occurred and its meaning for man. Subjective history is internal history, remembered events bound together by a thread of interpretation. It may include tradition, and tradition often is of deeper meaning for man

[2] H. T. Fowler in *Journal of Biblical Literature*, XLIX (1930), 217.

than purely objective history. We should not think, however, that when one is concerned with history all critical faculties must be suspended. Everyone interested in the writing and interpretation of history must, because of the compelling curiosity of the human mind, search for objectivity; but he must remember that objective fact alone is of little value.

We have thus far considered history as if it included only past occurrences. But an adequate definition of history must include both present and future as well as past. The past is only a small fragment of time, and history cannot contain a sense of destiny and purpose unless the present and future are comprehended within its scope. "Only a prophetic vision of the past," says Berdyaev, "can set history in motion; and only a prophetic vision of the future can bind the present and the past into a sort of interior and complete spiritual movement. Only a prophetic vision can re-animate the dead body of history and inform the lifeless static with the inner fire of spiritual movement." [3] No one, of course, can ever fully know the future, but to some degree the future is latent within the past and the fleeting present to him who has eyes to see.

INDIVIDUAL PROPHETS' REFERENCES TO THE PAST

The prophets were concerned with history in both of its meanings. They were "makers of history" in that they helped to shape events of their own time and afterward, not indeed as much as they wished, but always to some degree. They were also interested in history as it embraced the remembered past and the ultimate destiny of their people.

As we have seen, the sense of history arose among the Hebrews before the time of the great prophets. They were not responsible for its rise, but in their own work they did carry it on and deepen it.

Our first great prophet, Amos, made an appeal to history early in his book, emphasizing two or three facts which were to become

---

[3] Nicolas Berdyaev, *The Meaning of History* (New York: Scribner, 1936), p 41.

standard in the prophetic view. In chapter 2 he condemned the
Israelites for their sins of social injustice and harlotry, and said in
the name of the Lord:

> I destroyed before you the Amorite,
> Whose height was as the height of cedars,
>> And his strength as that of oaks;
> I destroyed his fruit above,
>> And his roots beneath.
> I too brought you up
>> From the land of Egypt,
> And I led you in the wilderness
>> For forty years,
> To inherit the land of the Amorite.
> I raised up some of your sons as prophets,
>> And some of your young men as Nazirites.
>
> . . . .
>
> But you made the Nazirites drink wine,
> And to the prophets you gave command, saying,
>> "You shall not prophesy!" (2:9-12.)

A little later he said concerning "the whole family that I brought
up from the land of Egypt":

> You alone have I known
>> From all the families of the earth:
> Therefore will I visit on you
>> All your iniquities! (3:2.)

This may sound contradictory to a passage quoted earlier, in which
Amos declared that the same Lord who brought Israel out of Egypt
also brought the Philistines from Caphtor and the Syrians from Kir
(9:7).[4] But it is not really so. Amos meant that, although God had
been concerned with guiding the history of many nations, he had

----

[4] See p. 51.

been especially concerned with Israel. They were a *chosen* nation, chosen not for superiority but for a special mission. Yahweh had laid unusual demands upon them, and, because they had failed to live up to those demands, they must bear an even greater punishment than other nations. The prophetic interpretation of the chosen-nation doctrine was always that from him to whom much has been given, much is required.

One sees in Amos not only this emphasis but a beginning of the stress upon the period of the exodus from Egypt and the wilderness sojourn as a time when God especially manifested himself to Israel and did for them something which placed them under lasting obligation to him. This period of history was to receive from the prophets increasing emphasis, culminating in the great use made of it by Second Isaiah.

Hosea had a greater interest in the remembered past of Israel than Amos, and went back to a more remote past than the Tekoan prophet. We may see the view which Hosea had of Israelite history by considering together a group of verses which are now scattered in his book:

> The Lord has a quarrel with Israel:
> > He will verily punish Jacob according to his ways,
> > And requite him according to his deeds.
> In the womb he seized his brother's heel,
> > And in manhood he strove with God,
> > Yea, he strove with an angel and prevailed.
> He wept and entreated for mercy,
> > At Bethel he used to find him,
> > And there used to speak with him. (12:2-4.)

> Jacob fled to the Field of Aram,
> > And Israel served for a wife,
> > Yea, for a wife he watched sheep.
> By a prophet the Lord brought Israel up from Egypt,
> > And by a prophet he was preserved. (12:12-13.)

When Israel was a child I loved him,
And from Egypt I called my son.
The more I called them,
The more they went astray from me;
They continued sacrificing to the Baals,
And burning incense to idols.
Yet I taught Ephraim to walk,
And took them into my arms.
But they did not know I had healed them.
With human bonds I led them,
Even with cords of love. (11:1-4a.)

Like grapes in the wilderness
I found Israel;
Like the first ripe fig on the tree in its first season,
I regarded your fathers.
They came to Baal-Peor,
And dedicated themselves to Baal,
And became an abomination
Like that they loved. (9:10.)

Hosea's vision of the past was wider than Amos' view for it went back to the patriarchal period. His reference to Jacob is to the patriarch himself rather than to the nation, and Hosea referred to his life largely in order to mention his sins. This patriarchal period was, however, only the "prenatal" period in the history of the nation. Israel was really born in Egypt. It was there that Yahweh looked on the people as his son, as fine and fresh as wild grapes or first-ripe figs, and spoke to them through the prophet Moses. Then they were loyal to him. But the defection from Yahweh came when Israel entered Canaan, in spite of all his loving attempts to train his child. As a symbol of the great wickedness of Canaan, Hosea used the incident which took place at Shittim, a strikingly abominable occurrence recorded in Num. 25 (see also Hos. 5:2). It was contact with the Canaanite religion which led to Israel's apostasy, termed by Hosea her "harlotry," from which he summoned the people to repent.

Jeremiah agreed in large part with Hosea in his interpretation of the past life of the nation. In fact, he probably derived his view from reading Hosea. We see this especially in the second chapter:

> I remember the loyalty of your youth,
>   Your bridal love:
> You followed me in the desert,
>   In a land unsown.
>
> .   .   .   .
>
> What offense in me did your fathers find,
>   That they strayed far from me?
> They went after emptiness,
>   And themselves became emptiness.
>
> .   .   .   .
>
> I brought you into a garden land,
>   To eat its fruit and goodly things,
> But you came in and defiled my land,
>   And made my inheritance an abomination.
>
> .   .   .   .
>
> For, two evils have my people committed:
>   They have forsaken me,
> A fountain of living waters,
>   To hew for themselves cisterns,
> Broken cisterns
>   That cannot hold water! (2:2b, 5, 7, 13.)

We have noticed earlier that in a reference in the "temple sermon" to the exodus from Egypt, Jeremiah said that the demands then made upon Israel were not for sacrifices but for moral obedience (7:22). In 15:1 he named Moses and Samuel as intercessors, but declared that God would not accept even their intercession for the people of his day.

Isaiah did not refer to the past history of Israel. This may seem strange, but the explanation is doubtless that he was more concerned with being a maker of contemporary history than in using arguments from the past in his appeals to his fellow countrymen.

Nor did Micah refer to the past; we have so little material from him, however, that we cannot say that he was unconcerned with this subject.

The prophet Ezekiel differed markedly from his prophetic predecessors in his view of the past history of the people. He frequently called Israel a "rebellious house," and he believed that Israel had been rebellious from the beginning of her life. He did not recognize a "honeymoon period" of faithfulness to the Lord, as did Hosea and Jeremiah.

Ezekiel's references to the past are chiefly in chapters 16, 20, and 23. These chapters use allegories which are sometimes carried to extremes that may embarrass a Western reader. They have doubtless been worked over by later commentators, but in general they represent the prophet's viewpoint. In chapter 16 Ezekiel says of Jerusalem: "Your origin and your birth is of the land of the Canaanites; your father was an Amorite and your mother a Hittite" (vs. 3). This statement, which is in general accord with the findings of modern scholarship, seems to ignore the Egyptian and wilderness epochs in Israel's past, but it may be that the prophet was speaking specifically —and accurately—of the city of Jerusalem. He went on to say that at birth Jerusalem was not treated as a child should be treated, but was cast out on the open field, where she was found by Yahweh— an Israelite Romulus! Jerusalem then grew up and when she reached maturity was betrothed and married to Yahweh. But then she became a harlot, going after Assyrians, Chaldaeans, and other foreigners. She was even worse than her sisters, Samaria and Sodom. This comparison between Jerusalem and Samaria is worked out in great detail in the allegory of the two harlot sisters in chapter 23.

We have noted that chapter 16 ignores the pre-Canaanite period of Israel's life. Chapter 20 alludes to this period, but the prophet states that even in Egypt and in the desert the people rebelled against their God, committing idolatry and other sins.

Ezekiel's view, then, of the past history of Israel was at variance with that of earlier prophets and with the generally accepted tradition. His chief purpose in the use of the argument from history was to prove that Israel had been corrupt and rebellious from the very beginning; she was of pagan ancestry, a foundling and a harlot. These are symbolical ways of expressing the great depths of Israel's sin; we have here almost an Old Testament doctrine of original sin. Ezekiel's hope, expressed most clearly in chapter 18, seems to have centered not upon anything that the nation might do but in the repentance and moral uprightness of individuals.

Passing from Ezekiel to Second Isaiah in the consideration of our present subject is like passing from darkness into light. Second Isaiah did not deny the sinfulness of Israel, but his references to history were mainly concerned with depicting the great acts of God in the past life of the world and the nation, acts which guaranteed his glorious deeds in the future. One of the strongest supports in this prophet's declaration of a complete monotheism was the argument that Yahweh was the only God who had both known and made the past history of the chosen people. He alone among the gods could foretell what in the prophet's day had already happened and what was yet to happen (41:21-24; 42:9; 45:21; 48:3).

Second Isaiah went back in his view of history to the very beginning of time, to the creation of the world by Yahweh. In beautiful poetic language he described the creation of the heavens and earth, and their inhabitants (40:12-17, and elsewhere). Yahweh was the only Creator, and the great offense in idolatry was that it was the worship of the creature instead of the Creator. From prepatriarchal history Second Isaiah recalled Noah (54:9). He referred to God's promise that the "waters of Noah" would not again cover the earth, and interpreted this as a token that now God was not to be angry with Israel again.

From the patriarchal epoch this prophet thought especially of Abraham. To Yahweh he was "my friend" (41:8); to the Israelites he was "your father" and Sarah was the one "who bore you" (51:2). The blessings to these two were recalled to be compared with the present comforting of Zion. The "first father" who had sinned

(43:27) might also have been Abraham, although it could have been either Adam or Jacob.

Perhaps the outstanding single event in the past of God's dealings with Israel had been the deliverance at the Red Sea. It was there that Yahweh "made a way through the sea, a path through mighty waters" and overthrew the Egyptian horses and chariots (43:16-17). From 51:1-10 it appears that this Red Sea deliverance had been interpreted mythologically as a combat in which Yahweh overcame Rahab, the great dragon. This interpretation would be appropriate in view of the fact that Isaiah of Jerusalem had sarcastically spoken of Egypt as "Rahab," a great lazy monster (30:7), but the allusion may be to a creation myth. The redemption of Israel from Egypt was used by Second Isaiah as a basis of hope for the new redemption which was about to take place (43:2, 18-21; 51:10).

From the later national history Second Isaiah recalled David. He promised that God would make an eternal covenant with Israel in accordance with the "sure mercies of David," who had been appointed a witness and leader to many peoples (55:3). This prophet recognized, however, that the nation had sinned again and again, and that this was the reason why God had allowed her to be despoiled in various ways and finally sold into captivity (42:24-25; 43:27-28; 47:6-7; 50:1; 51:17). But that was not the end. God was now preparing the way for the restoration and new redemption, and one of the agents for this was the Persian king, Cyrus, who was to do Yahweh's will even though he did not recognize him (41:2-4, 25; 44:28; 45:1; 48:15).

Second Isaiah's references to history show that he had the most clearly developed "theology of history" of all the prophets. His vision into the past and his knowledge of its events was more detailed. He used the past history primarily, not as Ezekiel had, to prove the sinfulness of Israel, but to prove the great power and goodness of God, who made promises in the past that were now about to be fulfilled in the immediate future. In his use of the argument from history Second Isaiah represents the climax of prophetic thought.

Jesus had little to say regarding the history of his people. When he lived the historical books of the Old Testament had been written, and most of them accepted into the canon. These included books which gave the prophetic interpretation of history. Jesus probably felt that his mission did not lie in the direction of teaching a correct view of the past; his attention was directed mainly to the present and future.

There are, however, a few passages in the gospels which show that Jesus realized the sinfulness of the Hebrew people in former days and believed that the men of his own day shared the guilt of their ancestors, or even excelled them in sin. One of the clearest passages is Matt. 23:29-36 (cf. Luke 11:47-51). There Jesus pronounces woe upon the scribes and Pharisees for their hypocrisy in building the tombs of the prophets and beautifying the monuments of the righteous, boasting at the same time that if they had lived in the days of their fathers they would not have been partakers with them in the blood of the prophets.

So you bear witness against yourselves, that you are sons of those who killed the prophets. . . . I shall send to you prophets and wise men and scribes. Some of them you will kill and crucify, and some of them you will flog in your synagogues and persecute from city to city, that upon you may come all the righteous blood shed on the earth, from the blood of Abel the righteous to the blood of Zachariah son of Barachiah, whom you slew between the sanctuary and the altar.

While this passage may reflect to some degree experiences of the early Christians, it may nevertheless go back essentially to the attitude of Jesus.

Somewhat similar is the well-known parable of the husbandmen in the vineyard in Mark 12:1-12. The husbandmen who slew the servants sent to them represent the ancestors of the Jews, but the people of Jesus' own time are represented by those who put to death the owner's beloved son.

Jesus thus condemned his hearers who felt that they were better than their forefathers. He may also have condemned that kind of pride which John the Baptist spoke against (Matt. 3:7-9). Among John's hearers were Pharisees and Sadducees who placed too great dependence on their ancestry and history. John felt compelled to say to them: "Do not think to say within yourselves, 'We have Abraham as our forefather,' for I say unto you that God is able to raise up from these very stones children to Abraham." Pride of ancestry and history was as evil as other forms of pride.

For the Christian, Jesus Christ has become both the center of history and the criterion of history. "Blessed are the eyes that see the things that you see," Jesus said to his disciples. "For I say unto you that many prophets and kings desired to see what you see, but saw it not, and to hear what you hear, but heard it not." (Luke 10:23b-24). Jesus was the fulfillment of Old Testament prophecy, not in the sense that he mechanically conformed to all of its predictions, but in the sense that prophetic religion came to full fruition in him. But he was more than prophet, establishing a new era under a new covenant. The Christian finds in Christ both the culmination of the history of the chosen people and the criterion by which events in history are to be judged.

THE GENERAL PROPHETIC VIEW

It should now be clear that one purpose of several of the prophets was to make the Hebrews aware of their past, not simply that they might know about certain happenings, but that their past might become a part of their consciousness of God and of their own destiny. Berdyaev has said: "In order to grasp the mystery of the 'historical,' I must have a sense of it and history as something that is deeply *mine*, that is deeply *my* history, that is deeply *my* destiny. I must situate myself within historical destiny and it within my own human destiny." [5] The prophets—Second Isaiah in particular—could say of the past events to which they referred, "This is *my* history," and they wanted the Israelites as a nation and as individuals to be able to

[5] *Op. cit.,* p. 16.

make the same affirmation. That is the real purpose of subjective history.[6]

The prophets were not interested in all happenings of the past, but only in a few outstanding events and periods which were to them great moments when God had manifested himself to Israel or times of shame when they had rebelled against God. The principal events which the prophets saw as great moments were the exodus from Egypt—including the Red Sea deliverance—the wandering in the wilderness, and the entrance into Canaan. Other events were sometimes referred to, such as the call and blessing of Abraham or the reign of David, but those events in the early life of the people were the great moments. The exodus from Egypt, when God rescued the Hebrews from slavery to a foreign people, was the first great deliverance and redemption accomplished under the prophet Moses; the wilderness wandering was the time when the covenant was sealed and Israel had a "honeymoon period" of youthful loyalty to her God; the entrance into Canaan and its contact with the sensuous, materialistic cults of that land marked the beginning of the decline away from God, called by the prophets usually "harlotry." From one viewpoint—that of Ezekiel—the whole history was one of sin and rebellion. But from another—that of Second Isaiah and, to a lesser degree, of Amos, Hosea, and Jeremiah—it was one also of promise. To several of the prophets the Mosaic period was the "apostolic age" in Israel's history, to which she should look for her ideals and whose loyalty she should seek to recover.

The prophets were certain that Yahweh was a God of history. He was not just a nature god, a deity who manifested himself through the forces of nature. He did manifest himself in that way, but his revelation also was upon the stage of history. Second Isaiah de-

[6] On the nature and significance of subjective, or "inner," history, see H. Richard Niebuhr, *The Meaning of Revelation* (New York: Macmillan, 1941), chap. ii. One should distinguish between the inner history of a religious community, which is the type of subjective history we are here concerned with, and history as written by a modern historian striving toward objectivity. In the latter's work a large element of subjectivity is likely to exist, even without his being aware of it.

veloped most fully the teaching that Yahweh knows all of history—
future as well as past—and that all is under his control.

Because history is under the control of God, it has a purpose.
The Hebrews did not think of history as being a series of cycles,
without ultimate meaning or purpose, as the Canaanites with their
nature religion probably did. In such a religion the annually re-
curring cycles of nature were dominant. The Greeks also conceived
of history as cyclic in nature, and so do many modern writers. To the
Hebrews, however, history was linear: the past itself showed purpose, and the past contained promises which could be fulfilled only
in the future.

This view of history involved the belief that Israel was a chosen
nation, with whom God had made a special covenant. Many modern
men, including Christians, do not like the idea of a chosen people,
for it suggests to them the doctrine of a *Herrenvolk,* a master race.
But this was not the prophetic view of the chosen-nation idea, even
though it may have frequently been in ancient times the popular
Hebrew view. As expressed first in Amos, implied in other prophets,
and worked out fully by Second Isaiah, the notion that Israel was
a chosen nation meant that she had been given a special mission,
that the discharge of this mission placed on her a unique responsibility, and that failure to discharge it would lay her open to special
punishment. Second Isaiah expressed this belief in his teaching concerning the Suffering Servant. The Suffering Servant idea must include the nation Israel, but it is not exhausted by the national interpretation.[7] It is an ideal which can be really fulfilled only in an
individual, and to the Christian has been fulfilled in Jesus Christ.
But one must not deny that Second Isaiah included the destiny of
Israel in the mission of the Suffering Servant (see 41:8; 42:19-25;
44:21). That mission was to be a witness and messenger of God to
bring the knowledge of him and his true nature to all the world.
Israel was thus to be a prophet nation, performing for the world the

[7] For a general discussion see my article "The Sources of the Suffering Servant
Idea," *Journal of Near Eastern Studies,* III (1944), 79-86.

mission given to the individual prophets on a smaller scale.

The prophets could see that the destiny of the chosen people was not fulfilled in their own day, but they were confident that the same God who had been Master of the past was also working in their own time and would continue to control the future. One of their chief aims was to convince their hearers that God had not confined his efforts to great moments of the past but was still at work within the world. And they believed that the promises made in the past could be fulfilled in the future only as men in their own day turned to God and sought to do his will.

CHAPTER VI

THE PROPHETIC VIEW OF HISTORY: THE FUTURE

To THE POPULAR MIND THE WORD "PROPHET" USUALLY MEANS A PERSON who predicts the future, a prognosticator. This is indeed one of the dictionary definitions of the term.

There are many reasons for this popular definition. One is that it states what men want to accept. Every man wishes to know something of the future in order to increase his own feeling of security. Renan once said that the Israelite was "obsessed by an unquenchable thirst for the future." This is a human characteristic, not an exclusively Hebrew one. It has been estimated by the Better Business Bureau that Americans spend about two hundred million dollars a year trying to find out what the future will bring. This is one tenth of what we spend for primary and secondary education, and two fifths of all the expenditures of all our churches for all purposes.[1] The desire to unveil the future is deeply imbedded in human nature and manifests itself with unusual force in times of crisis and change.

This popular understanding of the nature of the prophet is due also in part to the use which New Testament writers made of the Old Testament. They searched the Scriptures and found in them many predictions which they believed were fulfilled in Jesus the Messiah. They were essentially correct in doing this, and we should be thankful that in this way they maintained the unity of the Old and New Testaments as Christian Scriptures, but it is clear that in some instances they read into Old Testament passages meanings not originally there.

This popular understanding of "prophet" is thus not wholly without foundation, even though the prophets were primarily preachers

---

[1] According to Charles S. Braden, "Sectarianism Run Wild" in *Protestantism: A Symposium,* ed. William K. Anderson (Nashville: Commission on Courses of Study, Methodist Church, 1944), p. 120.

of the righteous will of God to their own generation. They were not unconcerned with the future, and they did make predictions. We have seen that a well-rounded definition of history must include future as well as past and present, and that only a true prophetic vision of the future can bind the future with the present and past in one unified movement. The essential question, therefore, is not *whether* the Old Testament prophets predicted the future, but *in what manner* they predicted it, and with what degree of clarity they foresaw detailed events.

USE OF THE PROPHETS AS PROGNOSTICATORS

It has often been maintained that the prophets foresaw in exact detail events which were to occur after them, especially in relation to the end of this world. Christian millennialists from the second century to the twentieth have often used the Old and New Testaments as manuals from which to predict the exact nature of the "end of time" and the date of its consummation. Biblical literalists have often insisted that every prediction made in the Bible has been literally fulfilled or will be literally fulfilled in time to come.

It should be noted first regarding this popular view that those who hold it usually make most use of biblical books such as Daniel and Revelation, and of only certain portions of the prophetic books of the Old Testament. As we saw above,[2] in the Hebrew canon the book of Daniel is not found among the "Prophets" but in the miscellaneous group called "Writings." It is properly classified as an apocalyptic work. Sections of the genuine prophetic books are apocalyptic in nature rather than really prophetic. There are unusually striking apocalyptic sections in the book of Ezekiel.

The apocalyptists were in a sense the successors of the prophets, but in many respects their thinking was different. Their view of history, both past and future, was more mechanical. The ethical was not as deeply stressed by them as by the prophets. They wrote

[2] Pp. 29-30.

in days of catastrophe, and their works were tracts for bad times. The apocalyptists had a genuine message both for their own day and for ours, but in reading their work we must beware of taking Oriental symbolism and imagery more literally than they themselves would have thought justified.[3]

This popular use of the Bible as a manual of prediction must in all honesty be set down as very often illusory. Again and again Christian interpreters of the apocalyptic portions of Scripture have made predictions and set dates which have not materialized. They have had to change their dates or have gone into disrepute because of their erroneous interpretations. It is unnecessary here to point out examples of such predictions, for everyone who knows Christian history can easily recall them.[4]

The careful student of the Old Testament can find in the writings even of the great prophets predictions which were not fulfilled and in the very nature of the case can never be fulfilled. A number of such predictions could be cited, but an especially instructive example may be seen in Ezek. 26:7-14; 29:17-20; and Jer. 43:9-13. In the first-named passage the prophet begins by saying: "Thus says the Lord God, 'Behold I am about to bring against Tyre from the north Nebuchadrezzar, king of Babylon, king of kings, with horses, chariots, horsemen, and a great host.'" He continues by describing in vivid detail the siege of Tyre, and ends by saying:

> I shall make of you a bare rock,
>   A place for spreading out nets shall you be,
> And you shall not again be built,
>   For I the Lord have spoken. (26:14.)

But Tyre did *not* fall to Nebuchadrezzar, and Ezekiel later frankly recognized this fact and made a new prediction about the Babylonian

---

[3] For a recent discussion from an intelligent viewpoint see Harold H. Rowley, *The Relevance of Apocalyptic* (London: Lutterworth, 1944).

[4] A number are conveniently collected in Shirley J. Case, *The Millennial Hope* (Chicago: University of Chicago Press, 1918), chap. iv.

king. In 29:17-20, which is dated April 570 B.C., he admitted that, although Nebuchadrezzar and his army fought valiantly against Tyre, they did not gain the city; Ezekiel therefore prophesied that Yahweh was about to give the land of Egypt to Nebuchadrezzar, and that Egypt would be despoiled and plundered as wages for the Babylonian army. The last verse declared that Yahweh would give Egypt to Nebuchadrezzar in return for the service which the king did for Yahweh against Tyre.

From well-authenticated sources we learn that Nebuchadrezzar besieged Tyre from 585 to 572 B.C., but was unable to take it, since the city was built partly on the coast and partly on an island half a mile from the shore. The king of Tyre, Baal II, eventually came to terms with Nebuchadrezzar and recognized his suzerainty, but the city was not conquered and destroyed, never to be rebuilt, as Ezekiel had foretold—a fact which he himself admitted in 570. And his prediction regarding the conquest of Egypt by Nebuchadrezzar was also incorrect! He was joined in this latter prediction by Jeremiah (43:9-13). We are not very well informed about the history of Egypt at this period, but we know that about this time Amasis took the throne from Apries. Nebuchadrezzar apparently left Tyre to go on a campaign in the south against Egypt, but it is entirely unlikely that Nebuchadrezzar did more than have a border skirmish with the Egyptians. He certainly did not take over the whole land.[5]

These passages should be deeply disturbing to those who think of the prophets only as foretellers of the future, and to biblical literalists. For here we have a case in which the prophet Ezekiel made an erroneous forecast, and in trying to correct it made another mistake, in which he was joined by the prophet Jeremiah! This is not, however, embarrassing to one who understands the true nature of the prophet, and it doubtless was not embarrassing to the prophets themselves. They would readily admit the possibility of erroneous

---

[5] Both of the Ezekiel passages are probably genuine; for detailed discussions, see I. G. Matthews, *Ezekiel,* pp. 97-98, 113-14; and William A. Irwin, *The Problem of Ezekiel* (Chicago: University of Chicago Press, 1941), pp. 190-91, 208-10.

predictions without admitting that their understanding of the fundamental nature of God and the moral law was likewise in error.

Finally, regarding the view that Old Testament prophets were primarily or exclusively prognosticators, we must remember that the great prophets themselves had to contend against popular fortunetellers and soothsayers in their own day. Divination has had a long history in Israel and other nations, and such charlatans were undoubtedly numerous in the prophets' days.

Isaiah (in 2:6-8) has words of condemnation for the house of Jacob, not only because they trust in material prosperity and military might and practice idolatry, but also, as verse 6 says, "because they are full of diviners and soothsayers, like the Philistines, and they clasp hands with foreigners." Here soothsaying and divination is considered wrong largely because of its pagan origin.

Again, Isaiah (in 8:19-20—a passage which is difficult of translation and interpretation, but whose main import seems to be clear) speaks against those who go to fortunetellers, especially necromancers who consult the dead in behalf of the living, and sets in opposition to such practice the true way of knowing God's will in the prophetic law and testimony.

Second Isaiah speaks vividly of Yahweh as the creator and redeemer who "frustrates the omens of soothsayers, and makes diviners mad" (44:25). Again, in portraying the downfall of Babylon, he sarcastically charges its inhabitants now to call for help upon those who map out the heavens, the stargazers, and those who prognosticate month by month (47:13). This is a condemnation of Babylonian soothsaying, but the great argument of the prophets against such practice was that it was pagan and not truly Yahwistic.

The book of Deuteronomy shows the influence of the prophets when it prohibits all kinds of divination, sorcery, necromancy, fortunetelling, and the like (18:9-22). The Deuteronomist declared that anyone who carried on these practices borrowed from other nations was abominable to Yahweh, and set in absolute contrast the work of the prophet, who was sent by God and given messages by him.

We should not fail to notice, however, that in Deut. 18:22 a test of prophecy is whether a prediction made by a prophet comes to pass or not.

Determining the Genuine in Prophetic Books

As we turn to the question, What *did* the prophets think about the future, and what *did* they have to say about future events? we come to the most difficult problem in the study of the prophets. It is easier to criticize those who have what seem to be erroneous views about the prophets than to state the true prophetic viewpoint regarding the future.

The problem is greatly complicated by a fundamental question: What portion of our present prophetic books was actually composed by the prophets themselves? In our study thus far we have had occasion frequently to consider certain passages as genuine, or authentic, and others as secondary, or late. The separation of the genuine from the secondary is of special importance in understanding the prophetic interpretation of the future. All the books of the great prophets contain forecasts of time to come, some of them forecasts of doom and destruction and others of hope and redemption. In some books, notably Isaiah, there is an almost rhythmical alternation of doom and hope.

There are two easy ways out of the problem posed by the presence of these diverse elements: one is that of uncritical acceptance of everything contained in the prophetic books as being from the reputed authors; the other is that of complete rejection of all prophecies of hope. The former is perhaps the popular view, while the latter is the method of some Old Testament scholars. Both of these are too facile. We cannot now, after generations of devoted critical study of the Old Testament, accept everything in the prophetic books as genuine. Apart from the moot question of logical consistency, many passages cannot because of their style and vocabulary be from the reputed authors, and many do not fit the historical situations in which the prophets lived. For example, it is one of the most assured results of modern Old Testament criticism, as well grounded as any theory in the history of literature can be, that Isaiah of Jerusalem did not write Isa. 40-55. On the other hand, it is equally naïve and uncritical to strike out from the prophetic books all passages of hope. This is to impose upon the prophets a strait jacket of logical consistency of our own making.

Unfortunately we have no absolutely certain criteria by which to distinguish the original from the secondary. It is impossible to agree with a recent interpreter of Amos and Hosea who has declared that the procedures and techniques used in distinguishing the genuine from the secondary in the prophets are as precise as the routine employed by the organic chemist in qualitative and quantitative analysis.[6] Would that this were true!

We may be able to understand better how secondary material came to be added to the prophetic books, and how such material can be detected by the modern scholar, if we try to imagine the process by which an ancient Hebrew book came into existence. In order to do this we must forget for the moment most of the things we know about the way in which a modern book is written and published.

In those days there were no copyright laws, and Hebrews had little if any pride of individual authorship. Plagiarism was an unknown word. Printing presses, of course, did not exist. Such writing as was done was confined to a very small group, for writing itself was a learned profession and the materials of writing were expensive. Furthermore, the men who first collected the words by and about the prophets—whether the prophets themselves or their disciples, we do not know—were not aware that they were writing Scripture. The portion of the Old Testament known to Jews as "The Latter Prophets," comprising Isaiah, Jeremiah, Ezekiel, and the Twelve Minor Prophets, was not definitely canonized until about 200 B.C., six centuries after Amos.

A book was not considered as finished when it was first written down; it was a living and growing organism. To use another figure,

[6] Rolland E. Wolfe, *Meet Amos and Hosea* (New York: Harper, 1945), p. xxi.

it was a literary magnet. In subsequent days and generations, editors and scribes wrote explanations, comments, corrections, and the like, sometimes on the margins—subsequently to be incorporated into the text—and sometimes within or after the original text. The purpose of many of these editors and commentators was to "modernize" the prophets, to bring them up to date for their own generation.

Many of the additions to prophetic books were made for the purpose of softening or even reversing the harsh judgments of doom pronounced by the original prophets. These often come immediately after such pronouncements of doom. However, as R. E. Wolfe, has said, "It is unthinkable that Amos and Hosea [or other great prophets] would have hurled thunderbolts one moment and handed out roses the next." [7]

Distinguishing between the original words of the prophets and the secondary additions is a complicated and difficult process, and even competent Old Testament scholars do not agree on the results. This, however, is not occasion for despair, but rather for frank admission that our materials are not as concrete and our methods as precise as those of the physical scientist. Some of the criteria usually employed are the following: vocabularly and style, poetic meter (to be used very sparingly), appropriateness to the historical situation both in events and ideas, and similarity or dissimilarity to material known to be from later times.

In seeking to determine whether passages bearing on the future are genuine or not, these criteria need to be used not singly but as a whole. There are in addition to these criteria three general tests, rules of thumb, that are of special importance in dealing with such materials: (1) In speaking of the future does the passage demand repentance of the people, or does it depict the future as being controlled by God wholly independently of man's actions and attitudes? (2) Does the passage stress the spiritual and moral characteristics of the future "golden age," or its materialistic aspects? (3) Does

---

[7] *Ibid.*, p. xix. Wolfe's description of the process of writing Hebrew books (pp. xvi-xxii) is well worth reading.

the passage show no preference for Judah or Jerusalem over Samaria and Israel, or does it show such preference? Generally speaking, those passages are genuine for which the first alternative in each case must be chosen.

One example will suffice to show how some of these tests and criteria may be used. The books of Amos and Hosea both end with predictions of a bright future—Amos 9:8b-15 and Hos. 14:1-8. If one will read these two passages carefully, he will see that in Amos there is no call for repentance, but in Hosea there is, the prophet designating the words which the people shall use as they come to God in humble penitence. The Amos passage emphasizes the materialistic aspects of the new day, especially the great fertility of soil which will prevail. The Hosea chapter emphasizes rather the spiritual conditions of the new day, the renewed favor of God being depicted in figurative fashion. Furthermore, the Amos passage seems to presuppose historical conditions which fit the time of the exile, not earlier, the fall of Jerusalem and the enmity of the Edomites during the exile being presupposed by Amos 9:11-12, and the exile from the Holy Land by the passage in general. For these reasons, and others, most critical scholars today believe that Amos 9:8b-15 is secondary and not the product of Amos' mind at all (vs. 10 alone may be original); yet it is entirely probable that Hosea 14:1-8 is from Hosea, as a natural outgrowth of his thinking.

INDIVIDUAL PROPHETS' VIEWS OF THE FUTURE [8]

Amos was a prophet almost wholly of doom, and we may find in his genuine words only a small ray of hope for the future. Many passages in his book sound as if he expected only unrelieved doom. He said that "a foe" was about to surround the land, strip it of its strength, and plunder the palaces of the wealthy whom Amos so strongly denounced (3:11). He declared that God was about to

[8] The estimates of each prophet in this section represent personal opinion and are of course to some extent subjective, but they also represent opinions held today by many students of the Old Testament. They are supported by considerable evidence too voluminous to be set forth here.

raise up "a nation" that would crush the whole land (6:14). Three times he forecast exile, once to a place "beyond Damascus" (5:27; 6:7; 7:17). The last words of the prophet in the book of Amos are:

> Behold the eyes of the Lord God
> Are upon the sinful kingdom,
> And I will destroy it
> From off the face of the earth! (9:8a.)

All of this accords well with his view of the coming Day of the Lord, which was in direct opposition to the popular view:

> Woe to you who desire
> The Day of the Lord!
> What will the Day of the Lord mean to you?
> It is darkness and not light!
> It will be as if a man fled from a lion,
> And a bear met him!
> Or as if he went home and leaned his hand on the wall,
> And a serpent bit him!
> Is not the Day of the Lord darkness and not light,
> Yea, utter blackness with no light at all? (5:18-20.)

The point of Amos' figures here is that the Day of the Lord was to be the precise opposite of what the masses expected it to be. It was to mean darkness, defeat, and tragedy rather than light and triumph, as the people imagined it.

All these passages appear to leave no hope for the future. Some scholars have thought of Amos as a prophet of unrelieved doom. But there are several verses in chapter 5 which hold out a degree of hope to those who turn to God and seek him in his true nature. "Seek me that you may live," says verse 4; "Seek the Lord that you may live," occurs in verse 6. This is summed up in verse 15:

> Hate evil and love good,
> And establish justice in the gate;
> Perhaps the Lord, God of hosts, will be gracious
> To a remnant of Joseph.

Amos believed that there could be a bright future only for those who would seek God and seek good—virtually equivalent phrases—but he was apparently realistic enough to think that the genuine possibility that many might heed his advice was very small indeed.

Hosea lived at a time when the world political situation was becoming more stabilized than in the days of Amos. Amos lived before the rise to power of Tiglath-Pileser III, who came to the Assyrian throne in 745 B.C. A man of great ability both as military general and as administrator, Tiglath-Pileser laid the foundations of the new Assyrian empire which lasted until the latter part of the seventh century. Hosea lived after Tiglath-Pileser's rise to power. That prophet, like Amos, often pronounced doom and predicted ruin and destruction to his nation. Israel had sowed the wind and was now about to reap the whirlwind (8:7). At times Hosea seemed to have been sure that it was Assyria who would be the instrument of punishment upon the Hebrews; in 10:6 he told how the bull-idol of Bethel, so fervently worshiped by the Israelites, would be carried to Assyria as a trophy of war to the "Great King." In other passages he forecast exile both to Egypt and to Assyria (9:3, 6; 11:5).

Hosea was much more a prophet of hope than Amos, and this fact arose from Hosea's understanding that the nature of God must include mercy and love as well as strict justice. In a very moving passage (11:8-9), which reflected some of his own experiences with an unfaithful wife, Hosea spoke of Yahweh as crying out:

> How can I give you up, O Ephraim!
> How can I cast you away, O Israel!
> How can I make you like Admah!
> How treat you like Zeboiim! [9]
> My heart turns over within me,
> My compassion is strongly kindled!

[9] Admah and Zeboiim were cities that had been destroyed like Sodom and Gomorrah; in fact, they probably played in North Israelite tradition the same role as Sodom and Gomorrah in the Judaean tradition.

> I will not execute my fierce anger!
> I will not turn to destroy Ephraim!
> For I am God, not man,
> The Holy One in your midst!

It was this understanding of God's nature that made Hosea a prophet of hope, but this hope was contingent upon the repentance of Israel. Chapters 6 and 14 contain verses (6:1-3; 14:2-3) that have been called "liturgies of repentance"—words set down for the people to use as they came to God in humble penitence—and they include or are followed by assurances that God will heal, forgive, and restore. In the light of these passages, we may have confidence also in the genuineness of 2:14-17, 19-20, in which the restoration of the nation is depicted under the figure of a bride led back to the loyalty and faithfulness of her honeymoon days. The first two chapters do, however, contain secondary passages (1:5, 7, 10-11; 2:1, 18, 21-23) in which the restoration is described in terms which are much more mechanical, with favoritism to Judah, and in figures that are typical of later eschatological hopes. Other secondary passages are 3:5 and 11:10-11.

Isaiah of Jerusalem held out to his hearers not only threats of destruction but also promises of salvation. His book has become a great repository for later prophecies of a hopeful character, many of them Messianic, but there can be no doubt that Isaiah himself was not a prophet solely of doom. To be sure, there are in his book, as in Amos, passages which seem to foresee only ruin. The closing verses of chapter 6, the account of his initial vision, seem to have in view only desolation, complete and absolute. Also, Isaiah's conception of the Day of the Lord was largely in agreement with Amos'; Isaiah thought of it as being, above all, a day of judgment upon the pride of man, a day in which man and all his high looks would be humbled and God alone would be exalted (2:12-17).[10]

---

[10] Translated above, pp. 69-70.

Isaiah believed, however, that a remnant would survive the general ruin, and that it would survive because of its repentance and faith. This belief is expressed most vividly in the name of his first son, Shear-yashub, which means "A Remnant Shall Return." In this name, "return" means not return from exile but return to God (cf. 10:21). Isaiah realized that the masses, or even a majority of them, could not be expected to have true faith in Yahweh, but he did believe that a small minority could be faithful and that they could be the bearers of faith, the witnesses to true religion. Isaiah, with his practical nature, even set about to create this faithful remnant in his disciples; he is the first prophet of whose disciples we have definite information (8:16). While some critics have said that Isaiah's doctrine of a remnant is not a promise but a threat, this cannot be correct. Certainly he did believe that *only* a remnant would be faithful and thus survive, but it *was* a remnant. In this teaching he advanced a thought which had been held very timidly by Amos (5:15).

It is possible that we should go further and state that Isaiah's hopes for the future were expressed also in his belief in the inviolability of Zion and in the future coming of a Messianic age. We have noted above [11] from the prophet's own words, that the former of these is non-Isaianic. The question whether he believed in the coming of a Messiah and a Messianic age is not easily settled.

The passages in the book of Isaiah which are frequently bracketed together as Messianic and possibly from the eighth-century prophet are 2:2-4; 9:1-7; 11:1-9; 32:1-8, 15-20. These present a fairly unified hope of a period which may be called "Messianic" in a broad sense, although in the first there is no mention of a Messianic person, Yahweh himself being thought of as coming to earth. In general, the Hebrews were more interested in a Messianic age than in a Messianic person. The last three of these do, however, envisage the reign of a righteous king from the line of David, who will usher in a period of peace and prosperity based upon justice and righteous-

[11] Pp. 52-54.

ness. The conditions of this time are thought of as being a revival of the idealized reign of David and the Garden of Eden.

These Messianic passages in Isaiah are "authentic" in a very profound sense, for they are a part of the authentic hope of Israel, whether they be from the pen of Isaiah himself or not. There are modern critical scholars who accept them as products of the eighth-century prophet. The arguments for their genuineness, however, are not entirely convincing, for the following reasons: (*a*) While detailed studies of the style and vocabulary of these passages have been indecisive, their style does appear different from the genuine work of Isaiah, being more clearly organized, having longer periods, and being less staccato than other passages generally recognized as Isaianic. Of course, it may be that these were composed to be read only, not to be spoken in public, and this could account for the suggested differences. (*b*) The passages emphasize that the righteous ruler is to be from the Davidic dynasty, and it is difficult to understand why this should have been stressed at a time when a descendant of David was on the throne. A desire for revival of the Davidic line is more likely to have arisen after its fall in 587 B.C. (*c*) The Messianic hope does not appear to be a natural outgrowth of ideas known to have been held by Isaiah, with his emphasis on faith and repentance, his doctrine of a remnant, and his teaching as to the Day of Yahweh. Connections with these can be shown, but they are not readily suggested by the passages themselves. (*d*) It is difficult to fit these Messianic passages into a known historical situation in Isaiah's life. Most of his messages arose out of specific conditions which are well known. Of course, they may be the "swan-songs" of the prophet, composed near the end of his long life. No one should categorically deny that they are from Isaiah's mind and pen, but it is difficult to prove that they are.

The younger contemporary of Isaiah, Micah, is the one prophet who must be set down, on the basis of his preserved writings, as a herald only of doom, absolute and irrevocable. His three brief chapters predict the coming of the Lord himself to bring destruction upon the land. Samaria is to become a ruin, and her idols are to be smashed. The land is to be parceled out to its captors. In a final outburst Micah forecasts even the utter destruction of Jerusalem and its temple. The reason for this inevitable doom is stated in 1:9: "Her wounds are incurable." This fierce prophet from the hills of the Shephelah may have occasionally held out promise to his hearers, but such words have not been preserved. Chapters 4-7, many of which are Messianic in tone, are from later writers, as also is 2:12-13.

Jeremiah's reputation as a weeping prophet would lead us to think that he likewise was a herald only of doom, but this was not the case. His commission to prophesy was a command not only "to pull down and to uproot," but also "to build and to plant" (1:10). Some of his earlier prophecies, especially those inspired by the peril from the north, seem to have in view the utter destruction of the land. "The whole land shall be a desolation," he says in 4:27. On occasion he considered every one of his fellow Israelites as sinful and worthy only of doom (5:1-13; 9:4-6). When later Jeremiah spoke concerning more specific situations he could hold out hope, but hardly the kind which his hearers expected. During the second siege of Jerusalem by the Chaldaeans, he set before the people of that doomed city a "way of life" and a "way of death." The way of life was to surrender to the Chaldaeans, whom Yahweh had commissioned to punish Israel; the way of death was to remain in the capital and die of sword, famine, or plague (21:8-10). Although some Jews followed this advice, it was naturally not heeded on a large scale.

More ultimate hope for the future is contained in Jeremiah's letter to the exiles, in his purchase, during the siege of Jerusalem, of a plot of ground belonging to a cousin, and in the "new covenant" passage which forms the climax and keystone of his teaching. We should observe, however, that his book does contain a Messianic promise (23:5-6; 33:14-17) and that chapters 30-33 include a number of promises of deliverance and salvation. For reasons similar to those which lead us to deny the Messianic passages in the book of Isaiah to Isaiah of Jerusalem, we must deny to Jeremiah the Messianic promises in his book (23:5-6; 33:14-17),[12] and a large portion of chapters 30-33 are clearly non-Jeremianic. The eschatological promises in those chapters are much more like those of later times than like the genuine teaching of Jeremiah.

Jeremiah, in his letter to the exiles (chap. 29), written after the first deportation of Jews in 598 B.C., counsels the exiles to settle down in their places of exile, lead normal lives, and seek the welfare of the land where they are, not hoping for immediate return to Palestine. He promises an eventual return, after "seventy years," and declares that God's ultimate plans for them are good and not evil; but he does not give any basis for thinking that the exile is to be of short duration. The exiles are not to be deluded by the false prophets who predict an immediately rosy future.

One of the most striking and most optimistic events in the whole life of Jeremiah is his purchase of a plot of land in Anathoth, as recorded in chapter 32. This occurred at a time when Jerusalem was under siege and Jeremiah himself was in prison. Information came to him that a cousin, Hanamel, was in distressed circumstances and was compelled to sell a plot of land, and that the right of redemption fell upon Jeremiah. This was in accordance with the law of redemption known to us from the twenty-fifth chapter of Leviticus. According to that law, land owned by a Hebrew could not be sold in perpetuity, but if a Hebrew were compelled by poverty to give up his land to a creditor, then it was the duty of a near kinsman, known as the "redeemer," to buy back the property in order that it might remain in the family. Jeremiah was obviously the nearest kinsman of Hanamel with sufficient funds to buy the plot. Jeremiah did this, even in prison, going through the legal steps necessary to the transaction. Jeremiah gave his reason for the action in verse 15: "For thus says the Lord of hosts, the God of Israel: 'Houses and

---

[12] See John Skinner, *Prophecy and Religion* (New York: Macmillan, 1922), pp. 310-19. It is possible that 23:5-6 is genuine. But, even if it is, Messianism does not play an important and really integral role in Jeremiah's thought.

fields and vineyards shall again be bought in this land.' " A more hopeful and optimistic action could not be imagined! With the army of the Babylonians surrounding the walls of Jerusalem, and himself a prisoner, Jeremiah was willing to invest money in a plot of ground in his home town, believing that it would prove a good investment. Such an action on his part shows a much deeper faith than that of the false prophets of the day.

The keystone of Jeremiah's prophetic message is reached in his prophecy of a "new covenant"—31:31-34. This has long been recognized not only as the finest passage in his book but also as a Magna Charta of personal religion which paved the way for the teaching of Christ. Some critics have denied that it is Jeremiah's. While it is true that it occurs in a portion of the book of Jeremiah which is largely secondary, and that the terminology may not be precisely that of Jeremiah, the passage as a whole can only be regarded as the logical development and outcome of Jeremiah's teaching. It is worth considering in full:

Behold, days are coming (says the Lord) when I will make with the house of Israel and house of Judah a new covenant, not like the covenant I made with their fathers when I seized their hand to bring them out of the land of Egypt—that covenant of mine which they broke, although I was their master—but this is the covenant I will make with the house of Israel after those days (says the Lord): I will put my law within them and write it on their heart. I will be their God and they shall be my people. They shall not again teach each other, saying "Know the Lord!" for all of them will know me, from the least to the greatest (says the Lord). For I will forgive their iniquity and not again remember their sin.

The new covenant does not envisage the giving of a new law, nor the revelation of a new deity. It envisages, rather, a time when there will be a new spirit and motivation for the keeping of the law, and a more complete and universal knowledge of the God revealed of old. This will involve forgiveness of sin and a direct communication of each believer with his Lord. How far this expression of a future hope is from those of a materialistic and mechanical nature so frequently met in the Old Testament!

Jeremiah's younger contemporay, Ezekiel, survived the disastrous fall of Jerusalem in 587 B.C., and that event seems to have made a great difference in his view of the future. As his book now stands, it is divided into three clear-cut sections: (1) the first twenty-four chapters, comprising largely—although not exclusively—pronouncements of doom on Jerusalem and Judah; (2) chapters 25-32, containing pronouncements of doom on foreign nations; and (3) the last sixteen chapters, concerned largely with hopes of future restoration. This division between the events before and after 587 probably corresponds to the nature of Ezekiel's prophetic ministry, as far as his own people were concerned. Before 587 he constantly forecast ruin and destruction, but he also wished to give his people an interpretation of the coming doom. It was due to their own sin and rebellion, which were so great that he could say, like Isaiah and Jeremiah, that Yahweh himself was fighting against Jerusalem (21:3-5). But he wished them to know that the punishment was governed by the purposes of God (6:8-10).

In 587 the predicted blow came. Jerusalem fell, Judah lost her political independence, and many more Jews were exiled. Ezekiel continued his ministry, either in Palestine or in Babylon, but it had a new note. The third division of his book contains many passages of hope of future salvation. Chapters 40-48 are a detailed priestly program of reconstruction, but we have seen that these are probably not from the prophet Ezekiel; they are too far removed from his vocabulary and his ideas to be a product of his thinking. Also, some sections of this third division contain highly imaginative eschatological predictions, such as chapters 38-39, the famous prophecies concerning Gog. This name may have been inspired by King Gyges of Lydia, but it has become a symbol of all that is evil and in opposition to God and his people. These sections too are probably later than Ezekiel; he was a more sober prophet.

Ezekiel himself pictures the future resurrection of the nation under the famous figure of the vision in the valley of dry bones (37:1-14). This was intended by him to symbolize the revival of the nation, not resurrection of individuals. "These bones are the whole house of Israel," says verse 11. Even Ezekiel, with all his individualism, could not get away from the strong Hebrew sense of national solidarity, any more than Jeremiah, whose "new covenant" was to be with the "house of Israel." This revival of the nation was to be attended, however, by the placing within the people of a *new heart* and a *new spirit,* instead of the old stony heart (11:19; 36:26). Ezekiel was a true prophet: hope and deliverance cannot come without moral transformation, whether it be wholly the work of God or the product partly of man's voluntary repentance.

The new Israel was to be a union of both Judah and Israel, for the division of the country into parts had long been a scandal to the prophets (37:15-28). Her shepherd and ruler was to be Yahweh himself; his rule would be in great contrast to that of the old faithless shepherds who did not really feed and care for the sheep under their care but thought only of their own comfort and safety. Ezek. 34:11-16 is a fine prose counterpart to the twenty-third psalm. The rule of God is to be actualized in the rule of "David" as under-shepherd or prince (34:23-24; 37:24). While this could have meant David reincarnated, it probably meant the revival of the Davidic dynasty. Ezekiel may have been the author of the Messianic hope which looked forward to a righteous king from the seed of David. In his reign there would be peace and prosperity (34:25-31, *et al.*). Ezekiel's hopes for future salvation were of a prophetic and not a priestly nature; the emphasis was on the new heart and the reign of righteousness under God. His hopes were charged with imagination, but it was a sober imagination, far removed from that which inspired chapters 38-39. His hopes were not transcendental, but were to be realized on this earth—on the soil of Palestine.

The last of the great Old Testament prophets, Second Isaiah, is the most satisfactory to deal with in a discussion of the prophetic view of the future. There are no difficult questions of authorship, except to those who hold that chapters 56-66 are from the same hand as chapters 35, 40-55—a view which seems unsound—and there is no question that this prophet was filled with hope for a bright future. His whole work is one of comfort and hope.

We have already noted that Second Isaiah had a well-developed theology of history. In his mind past and future were closely bound together. Both exist together, he said, in the mind of Yahweh, who alone knows past and future. The promises contained in the events of the past were to be brought to fruition in the near future.

Second Isaiah's poetry is pervaded with a sense that something *new* is about to take place. "Behold I am about to do a new thing" (43:19). "Sing to the Lord a new song!" (42:10). New things are about to be revealed (48:6), and Zion is about to hear good news (40:9; 41:27; 52:7). That which is new is the immediate redemption of Israel. Second Isaiah is the first Old Testament writer to use the word "redemption" in an eschatological sense; [13] to him the old deliverance at the Red Sea is but a prototype of the new redemption about to take place, sometimes likewise depicted as passing through waters (43:2, 20; 51:10-11). This new redemption is described by Second Isaiah partly in sober literal terms and partly in highly figurative poetic terms. Literally the redemption is to mean the release of the Jews from captivity in Babylon by Cyrus, and the return of other Jews from the many other lands to which they have been dispersed. All will return joyfully to Jerusalem, which is to be rebuilt and enlarged; the temple also is to be rebuilt. The land will be reconstructed and will experience prosperity. But this prophet's vision included more than the revival of Jewish national life and prosperity; it included ultimately the salvation of the world and the universal reign of Yahweh (45:14-25).

In more imaginative, poetic terms the poet-prophet describes the rejoicing and blossoming of the desert (35:1-2; 55:13), the raising of valleys and depressing of mountains to make a level highway

[13] See J. J. Stamm, *Erlösen und Vergeben im Alten Testament* (Bern: A. Francke, 1940), pp. 22-24, 39-43.

for the redeemed to walk on (35:8; 40:4, *et. al.*). Eventually the heavens will vanish like smoke, the earth wear out like a garment, and all of its inhabitants die, but the salvation of the Lord will be eternal (51:6). These descriptions, and many others like them, are not to be taken literally—as literal-minded Western readers have often taken them!—but as highly imaginative poetry. Second Isaiah is probably the author of some of the more imaginative elements of Hebrew eschatology, and even some later Hebrews took them too literally.

Finally, Second Isaiah believes that this redemption is to be accomplished by the coming of Yahweh himself (40:10-11). But Yahweh uses agents in the execution of his purposes, notably Cyrus, who can be designated as the "anointed" of God (45:1), and the Suffering Servant.

The view of the future held by Jesus of Nazareth centered around his teaching about the Kingdom of God. His gaze was almost entirely directed toward the future rather than the past, as we have noted. The idea of the Kingdom of God is a very ancient Hebrew idea, although the phrase is not found in the Old Testament. The belief that Yahweh was the only true king of Israel was very old, and most hopes for the future, such as those of Ezekiel, included the hope that Yahweh's kingship would truly be realized in the future time.

Interpreters of Jesus' teaching on the Kingdom of God, not only in modern times but almost throughout Christian history, have been sharply divided. On the one hand, many have believed that Jesus is best understood against the background of the apocalyptic writers of the Old Testament and intertestamental books. According to these interpreters, he taught that the Kingdom of God was to come in the immediate future as a visible, material kingdom. Support for this interpretation can be found in the gospel records, most strikingly—but not exclusively—in Mark 13 and its parallels, Luke 21 and Matt. 24. On the other hand, some have insisted that Jesus taught that the Kingdom is above all a spiritual and moral reality, already to some extent present to those who follow him. Support for this interpretation can be found in such passages as the much-debated Luke 17:20-21: "The Kingdom of God does not come with observation, nor shall they say, 'Lo here!' or 'Lo there!' For lo, the Kingdom of God is within you [or, in your midst]."

To deny the apocalyptic setting and background of Jesus' teaching demands the rejection of too large a portion of the gospel materials. And yet it is pertinent to our study to realize that on many crucial points Jesus was much more definitely within the *prophetic* than the *apocalyptic* tradition. In these respects he can be better understood as a successor of the Old Testament prophets than of the Jewish apocalyptists.

In the first place, Jesus' great interest—perhaps his primary interest—was in calling upon men to make the spiritual preparation necessary for entrance into the Kingdom of God. "Repent ye, for the Kingdom of Heaven is at hand!" (Matt. 4:17). This was the heart of his demand. Jesus taught that the Kingdom of God is indeed *God's* Kingdom. Man cannot bring it in nor compel its coming, but can prepare himself to receive or to enter the Kingdom, by repentance, humility, childlike faith, watchfulness, and moral obedience.

Secondly, Jesus was not a datesetter. "Concerning that day or that hour no one has knowledge, neither the angels in heaven nor the Son, but only the Father" (Mark 13:32). This occurs in the most strongly apocalyptic chapter within the gospel record. "It is not for you to know times or seasons which the Father has set within his own power." (Acts 1:7.) These passages should be a permanent rebuke to the modern interpreter of the Bible who knows times and seasons too accurately. The contrast between the spirit of Jesus and the spirit of the apocalyptists can be seen by even a superficial comparison of the gospels with the book of Daniel in the Old Testament, to name only one apocalyptic work. Jesus did not portray in symbols the rise and fall of empires in mechanical fashion, but called upon individuals to prepare themselves for the Kingdom.

Again, it is of great significance that in defining the nature of the Kingdom, Jesus stressed the moral conditions that prevailed within it. Nationalistic and materialistic aspects are not wholly lacking from the gospel accounts, but these recede into the background. Jesus wanted men to seek first "his Kingdom and its righteousness." One of the best possible descriptions of the Kingdom of God is given in two parallel lines of the Lord's Prayer:

> Thy Kingdom come,
> Thy will be done,
>   As in heaven, so on earth.

The Kingdom of God meant above all the doing of God's will on earth. Jesus never gave as precise and materialistic a description of the Kingdom as Rev. 21 gives of the new heaven and new earth. The ethical and spiritual description of the ideal state is not wholly lacking in the apocalypses, but it was not a prominent feature as in Jesus' teaching.

It remains to be noted, of course, that Jesus had a much closer relationship to the actual coming of the Kingdom of God, however that relationship should be defined, than the prophets of the Old Testament had to the future consummation which they predicted.

THE GENERAL PROPHETIC VIEW

We have seen that the various prophets held a variety of attitudes regarding the future. Micah apparently looked forward only to doom, and Amos virtually so. But Second Isaiah was filled with the hope of a new day and new conditions. We are almost correct in saying that there was a rising crescendo of hopefulness from Amos and Micah to Second Isaiah and Jesus.

From one standpoint this may be occasion for dismay. Does this variation mean that there was no *prophetic* viewpoint? Did they not see anything eternal in the changing fortunes of their people?

Far from being an occasion for dismay, this variety shows us more clearly the nature of the prophets. They were not idle dreamers who dealt in abstract, absolute principles far removed from the needs of men and their world; they were active participants in the life of their day, always keenly aware of human needs. Times of prosperity and false confidence demanded rebuke in strong terms, but times of sorrow and tragedy called for comfort and revival of hope. A great watershed in the prophets' view of the future was the Babylonian exile, specifically the fall of Jerusalem in 587 B.C. The prophetic predictions of doom and destruction were fulfilled, first in the fall of Samaria in 721 B.C. and then in the fall of Jerusalem. The doom was not on the cosmic scale predicted by the prophets, but their interpretation of the destruction as punishment of God upon sin was the significant matter. After the fall of Jerusalem, the times demanded hope, but that hope must be based upon prophetic terms, not upon shallow optimism. Jeremiah, Ezekiel, and Second Isaiah, who prophesied after the fall of Jerusalem, all expressed hope, but without compromising the prophetic demand for repentance and righteousness.

This variety in the prophetic attitude is not, then, really variety. They saw both doom and hope within the purposes of God for man. His judgment is a judgment not only of wrath upon sin but of grace upon sorrow. Both emphases are necessary in the well-rounded prophetic understanding of God's nature.

The prophets not only did not hold out hope based upon superficial optimism, but they had constantly to combat the rosy and naïve optimism of the false Pollyanna prophets who flourished in their times. These were extremely numerous, and had the public favor more often than the true prophets. Such were the prophets who, in the words of Micah, "when they are well fed pronounce 'Peace!' but declare war against him who pays not well" (3:5). Jeremiah seems to have been plagued by these false prophets more than anyone else; at any rate, he devoted more space to them than any other literary prophet.

A large part of the twenty-third chapter of Jeremiah is devoted to the false prophets. One of the bases of Jeremiah's opposition to them was their immoral lives. They committed adultery, he said, and aided in various crimes. But another basis of his opposition was that they prophesied prosperity in response to the wishes of the people rather than listening to the voice of God.

Thus says the Lord of hosts:

> Listen not to the words of the prophets
>> That fill you with vain hope!
> A vision of their own heart they speak,
>> Not from the mouth of the Lord,
> Saying continually to the despisers of the word of the Lord:
>> "You shall have peace!"
> And to everyone who follows the stubbornness of his own heart they say,
>> "Evil shall not come upon you!"
>
> . . . . . .
>
> I have not sent the prophets,
>> Yet they ran;
> I have not spoken to them,
>> Yet they have prophesied.
> If they had stood in my council
>> And made my people hear my words,
> Then they would have turned them from their evil way,
>> And from their evil doings. (23:16-17, 21-22.)

In a conflict with one of the prophets, Hananiah, Jeremiah declared that the true prophets of former times spoke only of "war, famine, and pestilence" (28:8). This involved exaggeration, but must have been true in the main. Jeremiah's own prophecies were largely of doom, but not wholly so.

The great objection which the true prophets made to this constant prediction of peace and prosperity was that it did not make any moral demands upon men. The call for repentance and for moral obedience to an ethical God was fundamental to the true prophetic view of the future. They believed that the future was in the hands of God, but also that it was in part determined by the free choices of men. If the prophets had been only heralds of doom, they would not have called for moral reformation; and they would hardly have called for repentance and reform unless they had believed some men were capable of it.

Amos called upon men to "seek good" and to "seek God." These demands were not precisely equivalent, but certainly seeking God included for the prophet seeking good and hating evil. Many prophets made a similar demand, and especially made the demand that men repent.

Another important factor in the prophetic view of the future is that they always viewed it with a strong sense of urgency. Prophets of doom spoke as if the doom were immediately imminent. It is coming very soon. On the other hand, the prophet could say: "The Kingdom of God is at hand!" *Now* is the time for repentance. The present moment is of critical importance, determining the future. It will not do for us simply to point out that when doom fell, it did not fall on the cosmic scale which the prophets predicted; nor that, whatever spiritual blessings individuals have enjoyed, the Kingdom of God has not yet come in all its glory. Chronologically and quantitatively a prophet may have been mistaken, but spiritually and qualitatively he was never mistaken. The present moment *is* always a moment of crisis, presenting man with the possibility of turning toward God or turning away from him, and bearing within it decisive significance for the future. An urgent moral demand, presented to nations and to individuals, is always an authentic and necessary element in prophetic religion.

We may well believe that the modern literal apocalyptists and datesetters are pursuing mirages, but with their deep sense of urgency—if it includes a strong moral appeal—they are far closer to the true spirit of Hebrew prophecy than the modern successors of the ancient Pollyanna prophets who can only pander to the whims and prejudices of the comfortable folk who pay their salaries. They are also closer to the true prophets than those occupants of modern pulpits who have become so completely conformed to our modern secularism that they have no word of judgment from the throne of a righteous God.

Because the true prophets made moral demands and summoned to repentance, we must say that their predictions of the future were usually conditional rather than categorical. They threatened doom *unless* the people should repent and in the hope of inducing repentance, they promised deliverance if the people did repent. This conditional aspect of their predictions is not always obvious, but frequently must be considered as implied.

We can now see that the prophets were concerned not so much with what *would* happen in every detail as with what *must* happen in view of the eternal nature and purposes of God. They dealt with fundamental matters, although they were in many ways children of their own age who spoke to their contemporaries. They spoke of God and his purposes, and they knew that he is not subject to change. They knew also the nature of man, with his sinfulness and his possibility of obedience to God. They wished to say, above almost everything else, that righteousness exalts both a nation and the individual, but that sin has its inevitable punishment. It is because they dealt with truly fundamental matters regarding God's nature and purposes, and regarding the nature of man, that the prophets *did* predict events of our age—and of every age. They did not predict detailed events and precise dates but proclaimed moral laws and religious truths valid for all time.

Chapter VII

THE PROPHETS AND RITUALISM

At the time when the great prophets began to preach, Hebrew religion had developed an elaborate ceremonial and ritualistic system. Although the Priestly Code, which contains the rules of the fully developed Jewish system, was not written until about 500 B.C., the earlier narratives and prophetic books reveal quite clearly that many of those rules were ancient practice. If we read between the lines of the pre-exilic prophets, we may see that the Hebrews were accustomed to make many kinds of offerings—burnt offerings, freewill offerings, thank offerings, cereal offerings, and many others. Some of their offerings were animals, while others were products of the field. Some animal sacrifices were wholly consumed by fire, but others provided the worshipers with sacred meals. Tithes were paid, new moons and Sabbaths were observed, and pilgrimages and festal gatherings were frequent.

All this required a great number of priests to offer sacrifices and tend sanctuaries, and a large number of prophets to perform cultic duties, perhaps mainly the giving of oracles. The number of sanctuaries in various cities, both open-air high places and enclosed temples, must have been large until the Deuteronomic reformation (621 B.C.), when sacrificial worship was centralized in Jerusalem.

Every reader of the prophets, especially of the pre-exilic prophets, must have noted that they frequently spoke of these ritualistic practices—usually in terms far from favorable. One of the most keenly debated topics in the study of the prophets is their attitude toward the sacrificial system and its necessary accompaniments.

Individual Prophets' Attitudes Toward Ritualism

Amos has much to say regarding the cultus, and his words are as strong as those of any other prophet. His bitterest denunciation is 5:21-25, where, speaking in the name of Yahweh, he says:

I hate, I reject your feasts,
  And take no delight in your festal gatherings.
Even though you offer me burnt offerings [1]
And cereal offerings, I will not be pleased.
  The thank offerings of your fatlings I will not look upon.
Take away from me the clamor of your songs;
  To the strumming of your lyres I will not listen!
But let justice flow down as waters,
  And righteousness as an ever-flowing stream!
Was it sacrifices and offerings that you brought me
  In the wilderness forty years, O house of Israel?

Elsewhere Amos uses sarcasm, inviting the Israelites to come to their sanctuaries—only to transgress and perform their own pleasure (4:4-5). He condemns priests, and includes the destruction of sanctuaries and altars in the general destruction which he predicts.

Hosea does not speak as specifically as Amos against details of the cultic system, except for idolatry. That sin he condemns again and again, calling the idols only the work of men's hands. He denounces the priests and false prophets even more plainly than Amos, accusing them of false leadership and even immorality (4:4-10). He says in 8:11-13 that Ephraim has multiplied altars, but they have become to him only altars for sinning. In 5:6 he declares that the Israelites "come with their flocks and their herds to seek the Lord, and find him not." The best-known passage in Hosea, however, is 6:6:

For I delight in loyalty [2] and not sacrifice,
  And the knowledge of God rather than burnt offerings.

[1] It is probable that a few words have fallen out here in the Hebrew, making a line which cannot now be recovered.

[2] The Hebrew word *hésed* is difficult to translate into English. It is often rendered by "lovingkindness," "mercy," "goodness," or the like. It really means fidelity to the covenant obligation, *pietas*. See Glueck, *Das Wort* hesed (Beiheft 47 zur *Zeitschrift für die Alttestamentliche Wissenschaft;* Giessen, 1927); and G. E. Wright, "Lovingkindness, Old Testament conception of," in *An Encyclopedia of Religion*, ed. V. Ferm (New York: The Philosophical Library, 1945), pp. 453-54.

Isaiah of Jerusalem might be expected in some respects to have a more sympathetic attitude toward the sacrificial system than Amos and Hosea. His famous inaugural vision (chap. 6) was inspired by the temple. Some of his words, as we have seen, can be interpreted as showing belief in the inviolability of Jerusalem. Yet no prophet speaks more scathingly and completely against the prevailing ceremonial system than does Isaiah in 1:10-17. Addressing the people of Jerusalem, he cries out:

> Hear the word of the Lord,
>   You rulers of Sodom;
> Give ear to the law of our God,
>   You people of Gomorrah!
> "What have I to do with your multitude of sacrifices?"
>   Says the Lord.
> "I am sated with burnt offerings of rams,
>   And the fat of fed beasts.
> In the blood of bullocks and he-goats
>   I take no delight.
> When you come to appear before me,
>   Who requires this of you—
>   Trampling my courts?
> Bring no more vain offerings;
>   Burning of incense is an abomination to me.
> New moon and Sabbath, holding assemblies,
>   Fasting and festival I cannot endure!
> Your new moons and appointed seasons
>   My soul hates!
> They have become to me a burden
>   I am weary of bearing.
> When you spread out your hands,
>   I will hide my eyes from you.
> Yea, though you pray long,
>   I will not hearken.
> Your hands are full of blood—
>   Wash yourselves clean!

Put away your evil doings
  From before my eyes!
Cease doing evil,
  Learn to do good!
Seek justice,
  Restrain the robber!
Give justice to the orphan,
  Defend the cause of the widow!"

In the light of a passage as vigorous and comprehensive as this, it is hard to think that Isaiah was really sympathetic toward the sacrificial system.

The prophet Micah had little to say that bears directly on the cultic practices of his time. He was largely concerned with social injustice and urban sins. However, in 1:7 he called for the smashing of Samaria's images, and in 3:12 he predicted unflinchingly that Zion was to be plowed like a field and Jerusalem was to become a ruin. Such destruction would, of course, include the temple and its ritual.

In Mic. 6:6-8 we have one of the clearest and most vivid denials of the validity of offerings as a means of worshiping God. This passage is probably not from Micah of Moresheth-Gath, as it seems to reflect conditions in the seventh century in the time of Manasseh. It is an inquiry about the proper way of approaching God which rejects sacrifice and offering and says that the true requirements of God are moral:

> With what shall I approach the Lord,
>   And bow before the high God?
> Shall I approach him with burnt offerings,
>   With calves a year old?
> Will the Lord be pleased with thousands of rams,
>   With myriads of rivers of oil?
> Shall I give my first-born for my transgression,
>   The fruit of my body for the sin of my soul?
> He hath made known to you, O man, what is good,

> And what the Lord seeks from you—
> Only to do justice,
> To love loyalty,
> And to walk humbly with your God.

Jeremiah in the seventh century began his public career after the Deuteronomic reforms.[3] It is quite probable that he never gave any sanction to those reforms, however much he may have approved some of their features which sought to establish a higher social morality. One of the great objects of the Deuteronomic reformers was to centralize all sacrificial worship in the temple in Jerusalem, and thus to abolish all the local sanctuaries where sacrifices had formerly been offered up.

If we keep in mind the great importance which must have been attached to the Jerusalem temple by the priests and by the people generally who followed Deuteronomy, we can appreciate the boldness of Jeremiah in attacking even this national sanctuary in his famous "temple sermon." This was delivered by him at the beginning of the reign of Jehoiakim, possibly near the time of that king's coronation ceremonies in the temple. It is reported in chapter 7 and chapter 26 of Jeremiah's book. The former chapter is more concerned with what the prophet said; the latter gives only a short summary of his words but a detailed account of his subsequent arrest and trial. Let us consider some of the salient words of this sermon, from 7:4-23:

Trust not in false words, saying, "The temple of the Lord, the temple of the Lord, the temple of the Lord is this!" . . . Will you steal, murder, commit adultery, swear falsely, burn incense to Baal, follow other gods whom you know not, and then come and stand before me in this temple which bears my name, and say, "We have been saved!"—only to do all these abominations? Has this temple, which bears my name, become a den of thieves in your eyes? Yea, I consider it as such! says the Lord.

---

[3] See my article "Jeremiah and Deuteronomy," *Journal of Near Eastern Studies,* 1 (1942), pp. 156-73.

Yet go now to my place at Shiloh, where I formerly established my name, and see what I did to it because of the evil of my people Israel. So now, because you do all these deeds, says the Lord, . . . I shall do to the temple which bears my name, in which you trust, and to the place which I gave you and your fathers, just as I did to Shiloh! . . .

Thus says the Lord of hosts, the God of Israel: Add your burnt offerings to your sacrifices and eat flesh! Yet I did not speak with your fathers and I did not command them, when I brought them up out of the land of Egypt, concerning matters of burnt offering and sacrifice; but this word I commanded them, saying, "Hearken to my voice, and I will be your God and you shall be my people, and you shall walk in all the way I shall command you, that you may prosper."

This is the strongest criticism of the temple and its cultus in all the prophets. Jeremiah spoke other words about the sacrificial system. For example, in 6:20 he said:

> What have I to do with incense from Sheba,
> And sweet cane from a far land?
> Your burnt offerings are not to my liking,
> And your sacrifices please me not.

Ezekiel, like Jeremiah, prophesied both before and after the destruction of Jerusalem by the Babylonians in 587 B.C. It is much more difficult, however, to assess his attitude toward the temple cultus than it is to understand Jeremiah's. If we accept the whole of the book of Ezekiel as being the product of a single mind, then we must conclude that Ezekiel was a priest (1:2) who had great interest in the restoration of the temple. Chapters 40-48 contain a detailed description of the reconstruction of the temple, its worship, and its priesthood. Many scholars today believe that these chapters are secondary to the work of the prophet Ezekiel, and this seems the most likely view.

Earlier portions of the book of Ezekiel contain passages in which the prophet speaks very much as his predecessors had spoken. The imminent destruction of the high places and altars is predicted in

6:3 ff.; worship at the high places and idolatry are strongly condemned in 20:27-29; 22:3, and elsewhere. Chapter 8 contains a particularly vivid description of great abominations said to have existed
even within the temple precincts shortly before the fall of Jerusalem
—a very objectionable image, idols or pictures of loathsome beasts,
and weeping for Tammuz by the women. Chapter 24 (vs. 15-27)
tells about the death of the prophet's wife and the injunction laid
upon him not to mourn for her in the usual manner. This is to be a
symbol of the approaching destruction of the sanctuary, for the
Lord says through Ezekiel: "Behold I am about to profane my
sanctuary, the pride of your strength, the delight of your eyes, and
the desire of your soul." (vs. 21.) This sounds much like the
prophecies of Isaiah, Micah, and Jeremiah in previous times. Ezekiel's
attitude toward the cultus may therefore have been similar to theirs,
although he does not state it in as unmistakable terms as they did.

The work of Second Isaiah came at a time when the temple had
been destroyed and the Jews were very despondent. Religious externalism in the form of elaborate sacrifices and ceremonies was not
one of the problems which confronted this prophet. His purpose was
to arouse the hope of his fellow Jews without the compromise of
prophetic ideals.

There is only one extensive passage in Second Isaiah bearing
upon this question, and it is ambiguous and capable of divergent
interpretations. This passage is 43:22-25. The true meaning seems
to be that God has not really required sacrifices and offerings; he
has not placed *that* burden upon his people as a prerequisite of forgiveness (see the second half of vs. 23), but he is ready to forgive
their transgressions and sins "for my own sake" (vs. 25). This is
not, however, a strong condemnation of the sacrificial system, and
it may be that Second Isaiah was on the whole more friendly and
sympathetic to the system than preceding prophets, considering it
inadequate rather than actually an offense against Yahweh. In his
great fifty-third chapter he uses a term from the sacrificial system
to describe the work of the Suffering Servant: he is to be a "guilt
offering" for the people.

GENERAL ATTITUDE OF THE EARLIER PROPHETS

The prophets from Amos through Ezekiel were the ones who spoke most urgently against the ritualistic system, but interpreters have differed widely as to their basic attitude and the purpose of their condemnations. Did these prophets intend to condemn only the abuses of the system, and if these abuses were corrected would they have approved of it? Or did they contemplate the complete abolition of the system as such? Before attempting to answer these questions we should consider three points which probably cannot be disputed by any interpreter.

First, it is clear that the ritualistic system was a source of joy and even of merriment to the people. "So you love to do!" cried Amos after issuing his sarcastic summons to visit the sanctuaries and bring tithes and offerings (4:5). Ezekiel spoke of the temple as the "pride of your strength, the delight of your eyes, and the desire of your soul," with the emphasis perhaps strongly on "your." The passage from Amos quoted above speaks not only of offerings but of festal gatherings, songs and lyres, and one gets the impression that he had in mind occasions of merriment rather than of solemn religious feeling. G. Buchanan Gray has said that the offerings which the worshipers made as gifts to deity were gifts which the givers themselves greatly enjoyed, not because they knew it is more blessed to give than to receive, but because their gifts lulled them into a false sense of security.[4]

It may be difficult for a modern man to enter into the frame of mind which would enable him to consider the sacrificial system as a source of joy. Largely because of our Christian heritage, we are accustomed to think of sacrifice as a serious and solemn matter. But we forget that many of the offerings which the ancient Hebrews made were not really "sacrificed" at all, if by "sacrifice" we mean an act in which something is given up by the worshipers at cost to themselves. Some sacrifices were made into whole burnt offerings, but many of them were actually consumed by the worshipers after

[4] *Sacrifice in the Old Testament* (Oxford, 1925), pp. 41-42.

having been dedicated by the priest or after the priest had taken his portion. In many instances, therefore, taking an animal to the temple to be sacrificed actually was little more than taking it to a butcher for slaughter. This may be seen by the fact that the Deuteronomic Code had to make provision for the slaughter of animals at home in secular fashion (12:20-25).

The truth is that many of the religious ceremonies were viewed by ancient Hebrews as little more than picnics where they could consume more meat than normally. With them, as with us, holy days had become holidays. When we realize that, for many American Christians, Christmas is primarily a time to have a big dinner and Easter a day on which to display new finery, we can understand a little better the feeling of the ancient Hebrew worshiper. The prophets must have realized that there was as little relationship between many of their picnics and true Yahwism as there is between a Christmas turkey and a Christian spirit of love.

Second, the prophets believed the religious ceremonies of their day contained no moral inspiration and incentive but had become an ersatz religion, a substitute for a well-rounded religion in which morality was basic. In most of the passages quoted above there is implied a strong contrast between the ritualistic system as practiced and the doing of justice and righteousness. In nearly every case the prophet sets forth an ideal which calls for a high morality instead of the elaborate ritual.

It is probably true that the priests and official leaders intended that the ritualistic system should promote individual and social morality, and it contained both ideas and words to this end. But such a system is easily corrupted and confused with magic, and it is evident that the prophets saw in it only a popular substitute rather than a genuine basis for high living.

Third, some elements of the system were considered by the prophets as actually immoral. There can be no question that, as a result of Canaanite influence, the Hebrews at times practiced physical prostitution in the name of religion. It is true that the prophets sometimes spoke of the false worship as a whole as harlotry, using the word in a figurative sense. But one of the reasons why this figure was appropriate was that physical harlotry was included in the cultus. There may well have been other elements which the prophets viewed as immoral, and not just in a sexual sense. The prophets frequently condemned the false prophets and the priests because they not only failed to hold up moral standards but aided laymen in deeds of unrighteousness and bloodshed (for example, Hos. 4:4-10; 6:9; Jer. 23:11-15).

These three observations may be correct, and yet we must ask whether the pre-exilic prophets believed the sacrificial system should be purified of its abuses or abolished entirely. Many scholars have taken the former view. They say that the prophets wanted the system to be moralized: it must contribute to a better life and not be a substitute for morality. This end could be accomplished only by eliminating the flagrantly immoral elements of the system and revising the attitude of the masses toward the ritual. This would involve also the simplification of the ceremonies and the elimination of pagan ideas and practices in favor of those which were true to Mosaic Yahwism.

Some scholars have believed that the prophets opposed a certain theory of sacrifice—the "gift theory," which was based upon the supposition that an angry deity could be placated by gifts, just as on occasion an angry man may be appeased by a gift. Certainly the prophets would have been against this crude theory, and yet they never suggest a better one.

The opposition of the prophets to the whole sacrificial and ritualistic system and practices of their day seems to have been absolute, and they thought it should be abolished as an offense against the God of Israel. This was the view of Amos, Hosea, Isaiah, Jeremiah, and probably also of Micah and Ezekiel. It was probably not the view of Second Isaiah; in his day, as we have seen, the problem raised for the prophetic mind by religious externalism was not acute.

It is difficult to imagine how any prophet could have condemned and denounced the system more vehemently or in more categorical terms than those used by Amos, Isaiah, and Jeremiah. Their words, taken at their face value suggest not purification of the system but its elimination. We may object that their attitude was too idealistic and impractical. But they were hardly "practical" men. The prophets were absolutists and radicals. They saw that the religious practices of their day were a hindrance to the true worship of God. They did not then sit down and calmly decide what would be a "practical" way of worshiping God, but denounced this evil with all their force. To them it was a root evil which could be removed only by drastic procedure.

Furthermore, it seems that the pre-exilic prophets believed that the religion of the Mosaic period was without burnt offerings and sacrifices and the whole round of elaborate ceremonial which to their minds was of Canaanite origin. To them it was pagan in origin and therefore in idea. The belief that the Mosaic religion did not include the sacrificial system is most clearly expressed in Amos 5:25 and Jer. 7:22-23, passages which clever exegesis has tried to distort or whose plain meaning it has sought to deny.

We may object that, as a matter of historical fact, the prophets were wrong in denying that the Mosaic system was without sacrifice. It is difficult to determine precisely what sacrifices were offered in Moses' day, but at least the Passover seems to be of ancient origin. The prophets may well have known literature which attributed elements of the sacrificial system to Moses. But the question here is not what *we* believe regarding the Mosaic age, but what the *prophets* believed. The canon of Scripture had not been fixed in their day, and they may have wished plainly to deny some of the beliefs held by priests and other prophets regarding the Mosaic age.

Modern discoveries and research have confirmed the belief that the Hebrew sacrificial system was largely of Canaanite origin. This has long been suspected on the basis of fragmentary evidence, and has been further proved by the discovery of cuneiform texts in a near-Hebrew language at modern Ras Shamra in Syria, the site of ancient Ugarit. These tablets contain ancient Canaanite religious literature of about the fourteenth century B.C., and reveal quite clearly that at that time Canaanite religion included many sacrifices and rites which were later incorporated into Hebrew religion. In some instances the names of the Ugaritic sacrifices are the same as those in Hebrew.

The prophets were, therefore, more nearly right than their contemporaries in viewing the sacrificial system as pagan and non-Mosaic, although neither they nor the proponents of the system were absolutely right on historical grounds.

GENERAL ATTITUDE OF THE LATER PROPHETS

The prophets who lived after the Babylonian exile were usually supporters of the temple cultus and its ceremonial. Haggai and Zechariah were mainly concerned with inspiring the Jews to rebuild the temple, which was still in ruins as late as 520 B.C., and their efforts were successful. Malachi severely denounced the people of his age for bringing to the temple unworthy sacrifices and small tithes. Joel mourns that certain offerings have been withheld from the temple. We may understand their position when we realize that in the post-exilic period the Jews were subservient to a foreign power, were a small community, and suffered many hardships. The temple could well serve as a rallying point for the community and could aid in maintaining its morale; and, once the necessity of sacrificial worship is granted, we must admit that prophets like Malachi were right in insisting that it be carried on in a worthy manner.

In the postexilic age there were, however, other voices which were raised against the emphasis on temple and sacrifice, voices of true successors of the earlier prophets. For example, the author of Isa. 66:1-4—who was not Second Isaiah, but probably a prophet living in the time of the rebuilding of the temple in 520-516 B.C.—denied that the God who made heaven and earth could be contained in an earthly temple, and that he could properly be served by slaughtering animals, burning incense, and the like. True service of God is in humility and contriteness of heart, and reverence for God's word. In the same spirit wrote the author of the fifty-first psalm, who may have lived in the exilic or postexilic age:

> For thou delightest not in sacrifice, that I should give it;
>> In burnt offering thou hast no pleasure.
> The sacrifices of God are a broken spirit,
>> A broken and a contrite heart, O God, thou wilt not reject!

We may finally ask, What was the attitude of Jesus toward the temple and the sacrificial system of his day? By his time the two portions of the Old Testament canon which Jews call the Law and the Prophets had become fixed. The laws regarding the temple, its priesthood, and its practices, and also regarding other ceremonies which did not center in the temple, had become fixed, although many details were still subject to dispute among the various schools of rabbis. The synagogue as an institution for common worship— without sacrifice—and popular instruction had been developed, probably beginning in or soon after the Exile.

It would seem that Jesus' attitude toward the religious practices of his day was not one of absolute opposition in the manner of the pre-exilic prophets, nor was it one of uncritical acceptance. As for the synagogue, he was nurtured in its instruction, customarily attended its services, and on occasion spoke in its meetings. His attitude toward the temple is not as easy to define.

On the one hand, Jesus seems to have attended some of the great annual festivals in the temple, as reported particularly in the Gospel of John. On one occasion after the cleansing of a leper he told the man to go to the priests and make the offering prescribed by the Mosaic law (Matt. 8:4; Mark 1:44; Luke 5:14). In other actions and teachings he appears to have taken the temple and its system for granted.

On the other hand, Jesus is said twice to have quoted Hos. 6:6: "I desire mercy and not sacrifice." Once this was quoted to the

Pharisees who objected to his eating with publicans and sinners (Matt. 9:13), and on another occasion to the Pharisees who objected to the disciples' plucking grain on the Sabbath (Matt. 12:7). One of the great acts of Jesus was to cleanse the temple, an action which brought down upon him the wrath of the priesthood and may have done more than any other single deed on his part to bring about his arrest and crucifixion. We must notice carefully, however, that this does not imply the destruction of the temple but rather a cleansing from the temple of its corrupt and commercialized features. Many strict Jews, especially those of the school of Shammai, may have supported Jesus in this action. And finally, we must recall that a witness at the trial of Jesus testified that Jesus claimed he could destroy the temple of God and raise it again in three days (Matt. 26:61). This testimony may go back to some saying of Jesus, but what its original import was we can hardly say (cf. Mark 13:1-2).

In view of this somewhat conflicting evidence, how can we determine the attitude of Jesus? It is likely that some of these conflicts are due to differences of opinion among the early disciples of Jesus. Modern study of the gospels has shown clearly that it is exceedingly difficult to recover the actual words and attitudes of Jesus, since these are given to us through the mirror of the early Christian disciples and the Christian community. However, a clue to the attitude of Jesus is afforded by an important saying of his recorded in the Sermon on the Mount: "If you are offering your gift at the altar, and there remember that your brother has something against you, leave your gift there before the altar and go, first become reconciled with your brother, and then come and offer your gift." (Matt. 5:23-24.) This has an authentic ring in it, and may give us the true attitude of our Lord. To his mind the offering of gifts on an altar in a temple was not in itself an offense to a holy God, but the worshiper must learn to put first things first. Being reconciled to one's brother through seeking his forgiveness is more important and must take precedence in time over the offering of the gift. The gift will be acceptable to a holy God only when it is offered in humility and contrition.

Jesus believed that the priest and the priestly system must be subject to prophetic criticism, and the essence of that criticism is that the moral must precede the ceremonial in importance. The ceremonial must never be a substitute for or hindrance to the moral, but must give moral inspiration and insight.

CHAPTER VIII

THE PATRIOTISM OF THE PROPHETS

IT WOULD NOT BE DIFFICULT TO ACCUSE SOME OF THE PROPHETS OF BEING unpatriotic. Indeed, several of them were not only accused but even convicted by their contemporaries of unpatriotic words and action.

The first of the great prophets, who was one of the boldest of all, was expelled from the town of Bethel on a charge of conspiracy against the king of Israel. We have the account of this in Amos 7:10-17. After Amos had been prophesying at Bethel for a time, Amaziah, the priest of the royal sanctuary there, became aroused and afraid. His fears were brought to a climax by Amos' declaration that sanctuaries and altars would be destroyed in the approaching day of doom, and that Yahweh would arise with a sword even against the house of Jeroboam, the reigning monarch in the northern kingdom. Amaziah hurriedly sent a message to the king to say: "Amos has conspired against you in the midst of the house of Israel; the land cannot contain all his words!" Then, in obedience to instructions from the king or on his own authority, Amaziah proceeded to order Amos out of the country. Contemptuously addressing him as "you seer," Amaziah commanded him to go back home to the land of Judah and make his living by prophesying there, never to come back to Bethel, for, declared the priest, "it is the king's sanctuary and a royal temple." Amos probably obeyed the order, for Amaziah had physical power on his side, but not without having the last word, in which he spoke his mind fully against the corrupt priest and his family.

Hosea did not come into conflict with the civil authorities, so far as we know. His personal difficulties were occasioned by his unhappy marriage. Hosea did, however, speak vehemently against the corruption of the king and his princes, and it may be—as we shall see—that Hosea opposed the institution of the monarchy.

Isaiah likewise did not, so far as we are aware, fall afoul of the civil authorities, although he gave unpopular advice to the king and his court on several occasions. Legend says, however, that he was put to death by being sawed asunder during the black reign of Manasseh. Micah, too, was never imprisoned or punished by the leaders— again we must say "so far as we know." Jer. 26:17-19 suggests that Micah's strong denunciation of Jerusalem and the temple was met by Hezekiah and his court not with rebuke for the prophet but with repentance and change by the king.

Jeremiah must have been considered highly unpatriotic by most of the people of his time. Early in his career he preached his renowned "temple sermon." The immediate result was his arrest and trial on a capital charge. A full account is contained in chapter 26. It was doubtless the priests and prophets, who had vested interests in the continuation of the Jerusalem temple and its services, who had him arrested, but it appears that in general the masses and the princes sided with the prophet. On this occasion Jeremiah was released for three reasons. One was that he himself exhibited great courage. He boldly declared that he was speaking only what the Lord had commanded him to prophesy and calmly said: "As for me, behold I am in your hands. Do to me whatever is right and just in your sight. Only know well that if you execute me you will bring innocent blood on yourselves and on this city and on its inhabitants, for in truth it was the Lord who sent me to you to speak in your hearing all these words." Jeremiah's courage was in contrast to the cowardice of another prophet named Uriah, whose message was similar to Jeremiah's but who, under stress, became afraid and fled to Egypt. He was brought back and executed (Jer. 26: 20-24). Another reason for Jeremiah's release was that some of the elders brought up the precedent of Micah, who also had predicted the destruction of the temple but had not been put to death by Hezekiah. A third reason was that Jeremiah had some influential friends among the princes, notably one named Ahikam, son of Shaphan.

Later Jeremiah did not fare so well. On one occasion Pashhur, the chief overseer of the temple, being displeased with his words, beat him and placed him in stocks overnight (20:1-2). During the final siege of Jerusalem by the Babylonians the prophet was arrested on a charge of desertion to the enemy and placed in prison (37:11 ff.). This was a completely natural action for the government to take. Jeremiah had constantly said, in public and in private, that the only hope of survival for the Jews was to cease their senseless defense against the Chaldaeans and surrender. When Jeremiah started one day through the Benjamin Gate of Jerusalem on a trip to his ancestral home of Anathoth, the guard quite naturally thought the prophet was acting on his own advice. He immediately arrested Jeremiah and accused him of deserting to the enemy. The prophet was taken to the princes, who had him beaten and placed in the house of Jonathan the scribe; later he was removed to the guard court of the palace. While he was in the guard court, his enemies succeeded in obtaining royal permission to put him in an old cistern. He was rescued from certain death there by the kindness of an Ethiopian eunuch, but remained in prison until the capture of Jerusalem by the Babylonians. Then he was offered safe conduct to Babylon and preferential treatment by the Babylonian officers, but Jeremiah chose to remain in the land to share the sorrows and sufferings of his own people.

Ezekiel is supposed, in the present edition of his book, to have been exiled by the Babylonians in the first captivity of 598 b.c., when Jehoiachin and many leading citizens were taken captive. Recent studies, however, make it appear probable that a great deal of his public ministry was in Jerusalem, especially in the period before the fall of that city in 587. It may be that he was among the Jews exiled in that year or in the third deportation following the assassination of Gedaliah. In any case, exile probably was not a very hard lot for most Jews, and Ezekiel does not appear to have been a direct critic of his own government's policies in the same way that Jeremiah was.

Jesus of Nazareth was considered unpatriotic by many people

in the first century. It is difficult for us to assess the degree of responsibility for his death which should be borne by Jewish parties on the one hand and by the Romans on the other. It is an indisputable fact, however, that crucifixion was a Roman, not a Jewish, method of execution. Jesus died on a Roman cross, and Pontius Pilate was doubtless glad to be rid of a disturber of the peace who might be a revolutionist. In any case, it was not the whole Jewish people who wanted him executed; probably it was the Sadducean priesthood that was most strongly opposed to him.

THE PROPHETS AND THE STATE

We shall better understand the attitude of the prophets toward the state, and hence their idea of true patriotism, if we bear in mind two important facts.

The first is that the prophetic right of criticism of the state was well established among the Hebrews. In our brief survey of the prophets before Amos we have seen that many of them were "royal" prophets—that is, advisers to the reigning monarch. They were retained by kings in order that they might consult oracles, or in other ways ascertain the divine will before important moves were made. The instances usually noted in the literature have to do with going out to battle, but the prophets were turned to on other occasions as well (see I Kings 14; II Kings 1:16). Undoubtedly the great majority of these prophets were sycophants and timeservers, telling the kings what they wished to hear. (Oracles can be manipulated by those initiated into their secrets!) But not all were sycophants. We have the names of a few who were of independent mind and dared to criticize kings at the risk of both popular and royal disapproval. Nathan dared to condemn the king for his sin with Bathsheba; Elijah denounced Ahab for the murder of Naboth; and Micaiah ben Imlah was courageous enough to go counter to the advice of four hundred other prophets and disapprove the projected military campaign of Ahab and Jehoshaphat. Other prophets whose names are recorded were independent in spirit, and it may be that there were many others whose names have not come down to us. The proportion of four hundred false prophets to one true prophet in I Kings 22 may be indicative of the usual proportion.

The important point for us to note here is that, however fawning most of the royal prophets may have been, the independent tradition and the right of the accredited prophet of Yahweh to rebuke the king were well established. The great prophets were successors of Nathan, Micaiah, and Elijah in this independent tradition. Isaiah and Jeremiah were most directly in the line of advisers to kings.

The right of the prophet to play the role of critic even to princes and monarchs implied that the prophet could usually do so without danger to his own person. To a large degree the prophet was a "sacred person" entitled to respect whether one believed him or not, for he was a representative of Yahweh. Therefore it is very rare that we read of the execution of a prophet. The only cases known to us in the Old Testament in which accredited prophets of Yahweh were put to death are those of Uriah (Jer. 26:20-24) and Zechariah (II Chron. 24:20 f.). An important factor in Uriah's execution was that he proved cowardly and ran away instead of standing his ground. Prophets were imprisoned, but this occurred as a rule only in times of great crisis when their preaching seemed to imperil national defense. The charge made against Jeremiah by the princes, on which the king agreed to his being placed in a cistern—which they thought equivalent to executing him—was that his preaching was weakening the hands of the soldiers and common people during the siege of Jerusalem (38:4). It was known that some Jews had followed his advice to surrender (38:19). Of course, the treatment meted out to a given prophet depended always to a large extent on the character of the reigning king. Hezekiah was a comparatively good king; that is probably why Isaiah was never even imprisoned. Zedekiah, who imprisoned Jeremiah, was weak and vacillating; he often wished to follow the prophetic counsel but was afraid to do so in the face of popular disapproval.

The other fact to remember has to do with the size and geographical position of Palestine and its natural resources. Palestine is a small country, roughly the size of Vermont and only a little larger than the largest county in West Texas. Its importance in world history has never come from its size. Furthermore, it is a natural land-bridge between the land of the Nile on the southwest and the section of the Near East comprising Mesopotamia, Syria, and Asia Minor to the north and northeast. People going on commercial or military business between Egypt and Babylonia usually passed through Palestine. It was literally at the crossroads of the ancient Near Eastern world.

This small, centrally located land was comparatively poor in natural resources. It was a "land flowing with milk and honey" only to men who had been slaves in Egypt and wanderers in a desert. The soil was undoubtedly much more fertile in ancient times than it is today, largely because the Hebrews practiced much better agricultural methods than most of the modern inhabitants of the Holy Land. The land was not so completely barren of trees as today, and the Hebrews by terrace farming and other devices were able to keep the ground fairly productive. But it was never one of the most fertile regions of the earth by nature.

Nor was it blessed with abundant mineral resources. Modern archaeological investigations have shown that there are iron and copper ore in the Arabah, south of the Dead Sea. These were heavily exploited by Solomon and some later kings. On the whole, however, the land of Palestine is not as rich in such resources as other nations of the Near East.

Because of its smallness, its lack of high agricultural productivity, and the scarcity of natural resources, Palestine could not be one of the great nations of its world and time from the political and economic standpoint. Many of the kings and leaders doubtless wished it to be, but the prophets saw with their usual clarity of vision that it could not be.

National Policies Condemned by the Prophets

Our problem in discussing the patriotism of the prophets is not to determine whether they were patriotic by the standards usually held in their own day and in ours—which are probably similar—but to discover their conception of true patriotism. Their conception must have differed from the one usually held; otherwise they would not have been persecuted by the governments under which they lived.

As the prophets exercised their right of criticizing the state, they found a number of policies to condemn. One was the policy of playing balance-of-power politics. Because of its geographical location and small size, a Palestinian state was constantly tempted to make political alliances with one or another of the great empires of the world, usually Egypt or the dominant power in Mesopotamia. Most of the prophets had occasion to condemn the kings who succumbed to this temptation.

Hosea frequently denounced this policy. In 5:13 he says:

> Ephraim saw its sickness,
>   And Israel its wound;
> So Ephraim went to Assyria,
>   And sent messengers to the great king;
> But he is not able to heal you,
>   Nor will he relieve your wound.

Again he says in 7:11-12:

> Ephraim has become like a dove,
>   Silly and senseless:
> They coo to Egypt,
>   They flutter to Assyria.
> As they go I will spread
>   Over them my net:
> Like birds of the air I will bring them down,
>   And chastise them because of their evil.

Other passages, such as 12:1, depict this vacillation between Assyria and Egypt, which can be verified also in the historical accounts of the period of Hosea in Second Kings.

Isaiah opposed foreign alliances on specific occasions when we know well the historical situation. In 735 B.C., after the definite rise to power of the Assyrian empire, some of the states of the West sought to raise revolution against the Assyrian emperor. Pekah of Israel and Rezin of Damascus were the leaders, and they sought to enlist the aid of Judah, under Ahaz. The Judaean king refused, and so was the object of attack by Israel and Damascus, who hoped either to bring him to terms or to place one of their own vassals on the throne of Judah. On this occasion the prophet Isaiah gave counsel to the Judaean king, recorded in chapters 7 and 8 of his book. Isaiah advised the king, as the word from Yahweh, not to be afraid of Pekah and Rezin, who were only "two tails of smoldering firebrands." If Ahaz would only have faith in the Lord, within a short time the lands of these two kings would be forsaken. It was at this time that Isaiah spoke of the famous "Immanuel" sign. The purpose of this sign was to verify to the king Isaiah's statement that within a few years—that is, before the child, soon to be born, should know the difference between right and wrong—the lands of these kings would be desolate. We know, however, that Ahaz did not listen to Isaiah. He trusted not in the Lord but rather in the Assyrian emperor, to whom he sent a large present of silver and gold in return for military protection (II Kings 16:7-9). In a little while Tiglath-Pileser came to the west, destroyed Damascus, and carried away many exiles from the northern kingdom of Palestine (732 B.C.). Judah thus obtained relief from the threat by Pekah and Rezin, but at the great price of becoming virtually subject to Assyria.

Although Isaiah had opposed the alliance with Assyria in the first place, he obviously believed that it was better to remain true to this alliance than to revolt, trusting in Egypt for aid against Assyria and thus reviving the old game of power politics. In 713-711 B.C. some of the Philistine cities revolted, but at this time the prophet went naked and barefoot for three years (chap. 20). He dressed—or undressed!—this way to appear like a captive and to say dramatically to the Jews that they would all become captives if they trusted in alliance with Egypt. Again in 705, when Sargon died and Sennacherib came to the throne, a number of vassal states rebelled, apparently led by Merodach-baladan of Babylon. Isaiah disapproved of the kindnesses shown at this time by Hezekiah to messengers from Merodach-baladan, as we are told in Isa. 39. Egypt also was involved in this coalition against Assyria, but Isaiah considered that land a false source of confidence (30:1-7; 31:1-3); he probably agreed with the Assyrian officers quoted in 36:6 as speaking of Egypt as a "broken reed."

Jeremiah later had to contend against this policy of reliance upon foreign alliances. During the early part of his career Nineveh, the Assyrian capital, was captured by the Chaldaeans and Medes (612 B.C.), and subsequently the Assyrians and Egyptians were most decisively beaten by the Chaldaeans in the Battle of Carchemish (605 B.C.). Jehoiakim was placed on the throne by the Egyptians, and remained loyal to them until the Battle of Carchemish. Then he shifted his fealty to Nebuchadrezzar, the Chaldaean king. But in time he tired of this and withheld tribute. This brought on the first Babylonian siege of Jerusalem, which ended in the surrender of Jehoiachin, Jehoiakim having died during the siege. King Zedekiah, placed on the throne by the Babylonians, was loyal to them for a number of years, but then rebelled; again Jerusalem was besieged. After a time the Egyptians sent an army which gave temporary release to the Jewish capital, causing the Chaldaeans to retire. But Jeremiah, who had proclaimed Nebuchadrezzar to be the servant and agent of Yahweh, saw that this aid was only short-lived and that ultimately Jerusalem would have to be taken by the Chaldaeans. His confidence in the final accomplishment of Yahweh's will is expressed vividly in 37:10: "Even if you should smite the whole army of the Chaldaeans who are fighting you, and there be left of them only wounded men, they would rise up, each in his own tent, and burn this city with fire!" Jeremiah saw with clear vision the weakness of Egypt, in spite of her pretensions to revival of her former greatness. Ezekiel apparently shared this view of Egypt, as we know from chapters 29 and 32 of his book, which contain oracles against Egypt, most of them probably from the time that Egypt gave temporary aid to Jerusalem. Both Ezekiel and Jeremiah, however, were overoptimistic in their prediction that Nebuchadrezzar would take Egypt, as we have seen above.[1]

The reasons why the prophets opposed the playing of the game of power politics by Hebrew kings are not far to seek. Their reasons were a compound of hard realism and bold interpretation of God's will. These two things were closely related in the minds of the prophets, and they would not have admitted a strict division between them. To them the will of God was the highest realism.

The prophets had good knowledge of the affairs of their times, and they often assessed the situation more realistically than the reigning monarchs and their advisers. They saw that Palestine did not really have a chance in its attempt to play the perilous game of power politics. It was bound to be crushed between the great empires of Mesopotamia and Egypt. In actual fact the siege and fall of Samaria in 721 B.C. were the result of the policy of vacillation between Assyria and Egypt which Hosea condemned. Judah bought a longer lease on political independence by paying tribute to Assyria and usually refraining from rebellion. Yet in 701 B.C. Jerusalem almost met the same fate as Samaria, and was saved only by the surrender of Hezekiah. The final downfall of the Judaean state was brought on by the revival of the policy of trying to play Egypt off against the Mesopotamian power, now Babylon. We can see today that the prophets were correct from the standpoint of realistic politics. It is often true that so-called dreamers are more realistic than so-called practical men.

The prophets' motives were not purely prudential. Their basic reasons for opposition to foreign alliances and power politics were

---

[1] Pp. 93-94.

religious. They knew that political alliance usually implied also religious alliance, or the acceptance of religious influences by the subordinate power. We have an excellent illustration of this in II Kings 16:10-15. There we read that Ahaz went to Damascus to see the Assyrian king, Tiglath-Pileser, probably after the conquest of Damascus by the latter. On this visit Ahaz saw an altar, doubtless of Assyrian type. He sent a pattern of it to the priest in Jerusalem, with instructions that an altar like it be made and set up in the temple of Yahweh in Jerusalem. Another illustration may be seen in the reign of Manasseh. That king had a long and peaceful reign, and was loyal in paying tribute to Assyria. But during his reign Assyrian influences became strong in the religion of the Jews, and had to be erased in the reforms of Josiah.

The prophetic objection to dependence on foreign alliances came also from the prophets' belief that such associations implied mistrust in Yahweh. Isaiah expressed clearly the prophetic view that salvation lay only in repentance and in resting upon Yahweh (30: 15); the feverish dependence on alliances and military measures was a denial of this view.

The prophets went even deeper in giving a religious interpretation to the political affairs of their time. While they rejected foreign alliances, they saw that Yahweh is able to overrule man's decisions. He can use foreign powers to punish Israel, but in turn he can destroy foreign powers if they too rebel against him and become proud. The best evidences of this are in Isa. 10, in which Isaiah calls the Assyrian king the rod of God's anger, but declares that he too will be punished in time for his pride; and in Jer. 27 and 29, in which Jeremiah calls Nebuchadrezzar the servant of Yahweh, but promises that in due time the day of visitation for Babylon also will come.

Closely connected with this opposition of the prophets to foreign alliances is their frequent denunciation of dependence on military weapons either for defense or for aggression. It is hardly correct to call the prophets pacifists in the modern, technical sense—that is, men who are absolutely opposed to the settlement of international conflicts by force and do not take any part which they can avoid in such use of force. We do not find in the prophets reasoned arguments against the use of force in international war after the manner of modern pacifist literature. On occasion Jeremiah, for example, could call upon his fellow countrymen to repair to the fortified cities to defend themselves against the peril from the north (*e.g.*, 4:5). Generally, however, the prophets saw the vanity and futility of trust in horses and chariots—ancient equivalents of tanks and bombers—rather than in God. This is most vividly portrayed in Isaiah's writings.

They opposed militarism as a false confidence and denial of trust in God. Isaiah said in connection with the events near 701 B.C., when Judah was conniving with Egypt to rebel against Assyria:

> Woe to those who go down to Egypt for help,
>   And rely upon horses,
> Who trust in chariots because they are many,
>   And in horsemen because they are very mighty,
> But look not to the Holy One of Israel,
>   And seek not the Lord!
> . . . .
> Now Egyptians are men and not God,
>   And their horses are flesh and not spirit.
> When the Lord stretches forth his hand,
>   The helper will stumble,
>   And the helped will fall,
> And all will perish together! (31:1, 3.)

Again he drew a sharp contrast between trust in military measures for the defense of Jerusalem and trust in the purposes of God:

On that day you looked to the weapons in the House of the Forest, and paid attention to the breaches in the City of David, for they were many. You collected the waters of the lower pool; you numbered the houses of Jerusalem; you tore down houses to fortify the wall; you made a reservoir between the two walls for the water of the old pool.

But you did not look to him who did this, and paid no attention to him
who planned it long ago. (22:8-11.)

Isaiah saw clearly also that war corrupts the moral standards of a
people. War should bring into a people a new seriousness of purpose
and the holding aloft of high moral standards. Actually, it does call
forth much heroism and courage. On the other hand, experience has
shown plainly that war breeds moral corruption and moral careless-
ness. This was expressed by Isaiah in words that have become in
part proverbial, spoken perhaps when Jerusalem was under siege:

> The Lord, Yahweh of hosts,
>   Called on that day
> For weeping and mourning,
>   For baldness and wearing of sackcloth,
> But lo! joy and gladness,
>   Slaying of cattle and slaughter of sheep,
> Eating flesh and drinking wine,
>   Eating and drinking [thinking],
>   "For tomorrow we die!" (22:12-13)[2]

In addition to criticizing trust in foreign alliances and in military
measures instead of in Yahweh, one of the prophets, Hosea, probably
condemned even the institution of the monarchy in Israel. There can
be no doubt that Hosea strongly condemned kings who reigned
during his career. In 7:1-7 he gives a picture of very sordid court life
in which the king is made drunk by his own princes. In 10:3-4 he
describes a condition of government in which the king is weak and
not respected and treaties are considered mere scraps of paper. In
8:4a he makes Yahweh declare:

> They made kings, but not from me;
> They made princes, but without my knowledge!

[2] These words may have been uttered by the prophet at the time when the people
of Jerusalem were rejoicing over the withdrawal of Sennacherib's troops in 701 B.C.,
but the precise situation is difficult to recover. An actual siege is suggested in 22:6-7.
At any rate, the words accurately reflect a "war psychology."

And again, in 13:11, Yahweh says:

> I gave you a king in my anger,
> And took him away in my wrath!

In addition to these, there are cryptic references in 9:9 and 10:9 to the "days of Gibeah" as a time of sin and wickedness. It is possible that this phrase refers to the lurid events of Judg. 19–21, or to the fact that an especially objectionable sanctuary was located at Gibeah. But, taken with the passages just mentioned, this phrase can best be interpreted as a reference to the reign of Saul, who had his capital at Gibeah. It seems entirely probable that Hosea took the same view of the monarchy as did the later writer—possibly E—in the books of Samuel. To the latter the establishment of the monarchy was not in obedience to the will of God but was a defiance and rejection of God in the desire to be like the surrounding nations (see I Sam. 8). To him and to Hosea, Yahweh alone should be king of Israel, in fact as well as in theory.

THE PROPHETIC CONCEPTION OF PATRIOTISM

The patriotism of the prophets, however, was not a purely negative thing. They did not spend all their time condemning the policies of their government and people. Their suggestions were sometimes positive.

They wanted the Hebrews, both people and rulers, to be a people true to Yahweh and to the covenant they had made with him. They wanted them to be a people of justice and righteousness in the sight of God. In order to be such a people, said the prophets, they must be willing to realize that evil and sin were to be found *within themselves* as well as within their enemies. This is one of the most important teachings of the prophets, hardly capable of being over-emphasized.

It is well known to the modern psychologist and to all who are intelligently interested in character education that an individual

has the possibility of progress in character only when he is willing
to face his own personality and character honestly and accept responsibility for his own actions. There is a natural tendency for individuals—as well as nations—to place responsibility on others rather
than shouldering it themselves. While it is possible for one to be
morbid about his own responsibility, there is a healthy way of
accepting it which is the surest foundation for moral growth. It
includes, among other things, what the religious man calls confession
of sin.

The prophets called upon the Hebrews to realize that their difficulties and tragedies were usually the result of their own sins. They
must, therefore, accept their own responsibilities. Even war in which
they were defeated by pagans could be interpreted as punishment
for sin, for Yahweh was the God of others as well as the God of the
Hebrews.

Everything said above, especially concerning the prophetic criticism of life in Chapter IV, has bearing then upon the patriotism of
the prophets. In order to be a true covenant people the Hebrews
must see that their sins are those of false leadership, with leaders
who seek to do their own will instead of God's; of narrowness of
vision; of abuse of economic power by the wealthy and too great
seeking of wealth by the poor; and of all kinds of pride, in race
or nation or religion or ancestry. These sins, the prophets said, must
be faced if the nation would be great.

The prophets were thus proclaiming to the Hebrew nation that
they should not seek to be a great nation in ways that were closed
to them; they could not be a great imperial power, or commercial
power, or cultural power. They must be true to the only kind of
greatness open to them by nature and by divine decree—greatness
in being a bearer of a unique revelation, a nation famous for its
moral and spiritual power.

It is one of the great paradoxes of history that the Hebrew people
reached greatness and were true to their own destiny only by being
in part blind to the advice given by the prophets. They sought to be

great in various ways that were impossible for them, especially by playing power politics. The ultimate result was that Jerusalem fell and the nation lost its independent life. But the last prophets were not those who lived before the Exile. Jeremiah and Ezekiel survived the destruction of Jerusalem, and Second Isaiah lived during the later part of the Babylonian Exile. These prophets, especially Second Isaiah, gave a prophetic interpretation to the sufferings of that nation that made them appear as something more than tragedy. By the grace of God they were made the means of the redemption of mankind. The nation was, to a great degree, the Suffering Servant; and the fulfillment of the Suffering Servant prophecy came in one who was born in this nation—Jesus of Nazareth.

The prophetic definition of patriotism, then, does not affirm that one's state is always right and that one must be ready to defend its every action. Nationalistic patriotism was, to the prophets, utterly false. Real patriotism to them was international and spiritually founded. It sought the *total* welfare of the people of one's own country, not of selected groups with vested interests, but it did not seek their total welfare at the expense of men who happened to live in other states. The total welfare of foreign peoples, too, must be sought. We find the highest patriotism in the universalism of Second Isaiah and, still more, in the teaching of Jesus concerning the universal fatherhood of God and the brotherhood of all men.

Chapter IX

GOD OF THE PROPHETS

THE PROPHETS WERE NOT SYSTEMATIC THEOLOGIANS. THEY WERE God-intoxicated men whose religion was God-centered. God was for them not primarily an object of thought and speculation but an object of intimately personal experience. Their teachings about deity do not constitute a carefully worked out system but are the result of insights that came to them in great moments of revelation.

As good Hebrews, the Old Testament prophets were much more interested in the deeds and demands of Yahweh than in the simple fact of his existence or in passive descriptions of his nature. They did not waste time in trying to prove that God exists. They took that for granted, like most men in the ancient world. The demand for proofs of divine existence is largely a modern demand. If faced with the modern necessity of proving his existence, the prophets would have said that their own lives, and the history of their nation, offered the best possible empirical proof of Yahweh. The history of the prophet nation, Israel, and the lives of the individual prophets, were to them living proof of the existence of a living God who revealed himself to men and cared for their fate.

It should be obvious that the prophets did not create the theology of the Hebrews—theology in the strict sense of doctrine of God. The prophets inherited much from Moses and from the leaders of thought and life between Moses and their own time. From the time of Moses they derived the belief in Yahweh as a deity who had made a covenant with Israel at a given moment. Yahweh was not, therefore, a natural deity—that is, one who had always been associated with Israel. It is possible that he had been worshiped from time immemorial by Moses' own tribe; we must admit, however, that the origins of the worship of this particular deity are wrapped in clouds of obscurity which have been only partially penetrated by the speculations of modern scholarship. It is clear, though, that the Israelites believed that Yahweh had chosen Israel, and Israel had chosen Yahweh, and a covenant had been created between them. This covenant entailed privileges and obligations for both parties. Yahweh was to be *their* God, with all of protection, guidance, and demand that was implied in that fact. On their side the Israelites undertook certain obligations, probably of an ethical rather than a ritualistic nature, embodied—so one is led to believe—in the original, brief Ten Commandments. The Israelites undertook to give to Yahweh whole-hearted and single-minded fealty, not worshiping or serving other gods. They also believed that the proper worship of Yahweh denied to them the use of images and required that they live righteously in relation to other members of the Hebrew confederation of tribes. Yahweh was in some manner peculiarly related to Israel, and in time to the soil of Palestine; but his power could be exercised also in Mesopotamia—as in the call of Abraham —and in the land of Egypt, whence he had led the Israelites out of slavery.

In the era between Moses and Amos—about five hundred years— much had occurred in the history of Israel and its religion. The nation had conquered Palestine and settled down there. The people had come in contact with civilizations that were from a material standpoint much higher than their own. Both progress and regression had taken place in their religious life and thought. The great problem was the relationship between Yahweh and the fertility gods and goddesses of the Canaanites. The prophets believed that they were largely summoning Israel back to the religion of the Mosaic era, but like all reformers they presented ideas that were both old and new. Their mission was actually not so much to present new ideas of God as to correct at some points mistaken notions and to deepen and widen the Hebrew understanding of God's nature. They wished to deepen the Hebrew experience of God and to widen the area of life over which the Hebrews would recognize his sovereignty.

ONE GOD

The prophets were monotheists, from Amos on. They believed that there was only one God, Yahweh, and that he was one. Prophetic monotheism is most clearly and thoroughly presented in the writing of Second Isaiah, but it is difficult to believe that any of them, from Amos through Ezekiel, were other than monotheists. They had not, like Second Isaiah, observed and developed the various implications of monotheism, but a belief that Yahweh was the only God was implied in their theology.

Hebrew monotheism was not arrived at by speculation of a philosophical nature, nor by Yahweh's conquest of the other gods of a pantheon. It was reached by the revelation to the prophets, and their discovery, that Yahweh was *all-sufficient* in his power and in his demands so that the Israelites, and ultimately all men, needed no other deity. Prophetic monotheism, which reached its full development in Second Isaiah, came to the Hebrews in their struggle with Canaanite Baalism and Philistine religion, and with the Egyptians, Assyrians, and Babylonians. The prophets came to believe that Yahweh was the God of Assyria, of Egypt, of Philistia—of all nations which came within the ken of the Hebrews—as well as of Israel. Amos pointed out that Yahweh made moral demands on the surrounding nations as well as on Israel, and punished them for failure to live up to those demands. Isaiah was sure that Yahweh guided Assyria, Jeremiah that he controlled Chaldaea, and Second Isaiah that he used Cyrus. There was no room for national deities in prophetic theology.

The prophets believed that Yahweh was the planner and controller of history, and also a deity who manifested his glory in nature, controlling it and using it for his purposes. He was the God both of the nation and of the individual. He was the creator of the ends of the earth, but he had a care for individual souls. He was God both of wrath and of mercy, of justice and of love. He was the author of both good and evil, the creator of darkness as well as of light (Isa 45:7) The dualism which conceived of Satan as a force of evil and darkness in opposition to God arose after the time of the great prophets.

A Moral God

An insistent feature of the prophets' understanding of God is that his requirements are ethical rather than ritualistic, and that his own nature is moral.

We have already seen that most of the great prophets of the Old Testament were absolute in their belief that the true demands of Yahweh were not for sacrifice and rite but rather for righteous conduct and right living in human relations. The teaching of Jesus resolved this conflict, but he nevertheless placed the moral before the ceremonial, and must surely have believed that any rite which was considered a substitute for or hindrance to morality was an insult to a righteous deity.

One of the reasons why the prophets insisted so strongly that the only, or the primary, demands of God are for ethical obedience was their belief that God is himself of a moral, rational nature. God *is* moral, they said, and thus has the right to make moral demands.

Before the time of Amos many Israelites apparently believed that Yahweh might do immoral and irrational things simply because he was a deity. There are two extreme examples of this in early literature. Exod. 4:24-26 contains the strange story of how Yahweh met Moses at a lodging place and sought to kill him, apparently because Moses had not been circumcised. The anger of Yahweh was appeased only when Zipporah, Moses' wife, cut off the foreskin of her son and thus performed a substitute circumcision of her husband. This is an obscure story which at best illustrates belief in a highly irrational deity.

The fourteenth chapter of First Samuel has another extreme illustration of an irrational and immoral conception of God. During a battle with the Philistines, Saul pronounced a curse on any of his warriors who should taste food before evening. But his own son, not knowing of this interdict, ate of some honey, and his sin brought misfortune upon Saul and the Hebrews. Subsequently it was revealed by an oracle that Jonathan was the culprit, and his father was on the point of putting him to death when he was ransomed by the people. This whole story has a strong religious basis, and shows that the people at this time believed Yahweh could, through the king, make demands of an immoral nature.

Such an understanding of the nature of God cannot be found in the prophets. They believed that his punishment of men is inflicted for breaking the moral law, not for violating irrational taboos or ritualistic requirements. This is because, as Jeremiah said, God practices lovingkindness, justice, and righteousness, and delights in such things (9:24).

The prophets' teaching that God is moral and demands morality of men challenges men to be Godlike in their living. It does not mean that they are to set themselves up as God, or above God; to the prophets a major sin was pride, the essence of which is to make oneself God. Men are expected to be like God not in power but rather in character. They are challenged to consider the moral character of God as their own ideal of moral personality. We are reminded of the demand of Jesus that men be "perfect" even as their heavenly Father is "perfect" (Matt. 5:48). This means, as Frederick C. Grant has well shown, that men are to have integrity in all their dealings as God has integrity in his own dealings with men.[1] Grant correctly interprets this saying of Jesus on the basis of the Old Testament, using especially Deut. 18:9-14.

The idea that Yahweh was moral did not conflict with the belief that he was the author of both good and evil. He was the author, the prophets believed, of misfortune as well as of good fortune, of darkness as well as of light, of good and of evil. But this belief did not mean to them that Yahweh's own actions might be evil, contrary to his own moral law. The prophetic belief in God's creation of evil as well as good was in accord with their belief in his absolute power and their unwillingness to attribute anything in the

[1] *The Earliest Gospel* (New York and Nashville: Abingdon-Cokesbury, 1943), pp. 218-23.

world to a will other than his own. This did not, however, deny man's own freedom of choice.

A SPIRITUAL PERSON

The prophets believed that Yahweh was a spirit and a person, or —to use a single phrase—a spiritual person. They did not, of course, originate this belief, but they did carry it to its most natural conclusions.

The Hebrews gloried in the thought that Yahweh was a person. They were not ashamed that he was, to use a modern expression, anthropomorphic. Negatively, this meant that he was not an astral deity, a personification of sun, moon, or stars, like many Assyrian and Babylonian deities; not an animal deity, like many gods of Egypt; and not an abstraction of certain qualities. Positively, the Hebrews believed he was a living, active God who could best be described by analogy with human beings at their best. He was a decision-making person who had communication with and care for decision-making persons on this earth.

The God of the prophets was, however, a transcendent God, far above man and far above man's complete understanding of him. This is most vividly expressed in the classic words of Second Isaiah:

> For my thoughts are not your thoughts,
>   And your ways are not my ways (says the Lord);
> For, as the heavens are higher than the earth,
> So are my ways higher than your ways,
>   And my thoughts than your thoughts. (55:8-9.)

The transcendence of God above man did not cause the prophets to despair of knowing God at all. They believed that they could not know him entirely, but certainly maintained that the revelation of his nature which they had was valid and dependable. The very idea of prophecy, of God's speaking to man through chosen individuals, required this.

Yahweh was conceived as a *spiritual* person. The Old Testament never says in so many words, as the New Testament does, that God *is* spirit (John 4:24), but it repeatedly implies that God is spirit, that he is of spiritual substance. The clearest expression is in Isa. 31:3:

> The Egyptians are men and not God,
> And their horses flesh and not spirit.

The purpose of this verse in its context [2] is to contrast God as spirit with the Egyptians and their horses, which are mere flesh. There is here the emphasis, found usually in the Old Testament, that spirit is powerful. The Hebrews used the same word for both "wind" and "spirit," and were impressed by the power which spirit could exert. Of course, spirit, like wind, was considered to be pervasive and mysterious. Also, the word for spirit sometimes was used for strong emotion. But the chief emphasis was on the strength associated with the word.

It may be that the Hebrews did not conceive of spirit as being immaterial but rather as a very refined type of matter. We cannot prove this by citing passages, but it seems in accord with Hebrew thinking in general. They apparently believed that God was made of spirit-substance, and man was a combination of spirit-substance and "dust," or "flesh." Man thus shared spirit with God, but by contrast with God was very weak, constantly needing his strength as support.

A great practical consequence for the prophets in the teaching that Yahweh was a spiritual person was their opposition to idolatry. The prohibition against idolatry may go back to Moses, but the masses undoubtedly practiced on a wide scale a form of idolatry which was most distasteful to the prophets, especially to Hosea and Second Isaiah.

Hosea poured scorn and ridicule upon idols, especially the bull-image of Samaria. To him the idols were only so much silver, gold, or wood—the products of human artisans. He could scornfully call

---

[2] Considered above, p. 144.

the image in Samaria a bull and say, "A workman made it, and it is no god" (8:6). He predicted that it would be taken as a trophy of war into exile to Assyria (10:6). He ridiculed the worshipers by crying out "Men kiss calves!" (13:2).

The polemic of Second Isaiah is in very much the same vein, but is more philosophical. In vivid detail he describes how workmen make idols and states that these idols are worth no more than the materials which make them up (40:19-20; 41:6-7; 44:9-20). An idol is a created thing, and must be cared for and borne around by its worshipers. Yahweh, the God of Israel, is, on the other hand, a creator and has borne Israel as one bears a burden (46:3-4). These prophets have given the classic definition of idolatry: it is worship of the creature instead of the creator. Idolatry is a denial not only of the spirituality of God but of his creative and sustaining work for man and his world.

CONTROLLER OF NATURE AND HISTORY

The prophetic view of God saw him as combining within his nature a number of qualities which might be thought of as antithetic or separate, but all of which were necessary to his being a deity adequate and sufficient for man. One of the most important of these combinations was the belief that Yahweh was the controller both of nature and of history.

Second Isaiah taught that only Yahweh knew past and future; we may infer that the thought that all of history existed within the mind of God. The prophets taught that Yahweh had controlled the past, was working in the present, and would guide the future. It may be that we who are in the Jewish and Christian traditions are so accustomed to this idea that its significance is lost on us; but such a belief was surely not common in the ancient world, and those of us who have inherited the Jewish and Christian traditions owe this idea primarily to the prophets.

But Yahweh was conceived of as also controlling nature and manifesting himself through it. Yahweh was not a personification of nature as a whole, or of some part of it; he was not caught within the endless cycle of birth, growth, and death which occurs in vegetation and animal life. Yahweh was considered to be a person who directly controlled the world of nature as well as the stage of history.

From the time of Moses, or even earlier, Yahweh had been associated with nature, especially with the violent and destructive forces such as storms and earthquakes. It may be that originally Yahweh was, as one scholar has suggested, a South Arabic storm deity.[3] At any rate, his power was manifested to the Hebrews in their early history especially in destructive natural elements. When the Hebrews entered Palestine and came in contact with Canaanite civilization, they found a religion whose principal gods and goddesses were connected with fertility and with the life-giving forces of nature. Many Hebrews doubtless felt they had to worship those deities in order to have fertility for their crops and herds. In time, though, the leaders of Yahwism proclaimed clearly that Yahweh had power also over the gentler, fertility-producing forces. Elijah proved that Yahweh could withhold rain and cause famine, and in his own time send rain. Perhaps the underlying significance of Elijah's vision on Horeb (I Kings 19), in which Yahweh was not in the wind, earthquake, or fire but rather in the "sound of gentle stillness," was that Yahweh was to be found in the gentle elements of nature. Hosea stated unmistakably that Yahweh was the deity who gave to Israel her grain, wine, and oil (Hosea 2:8).

The prophets were not interested, however, simply in the fact that Yahweh could control all of nature, but in teaching that events in nature could be used by Yahweh as the means of his judgments upon men. For example, Amos 4:6-12 is a long poem in which the prophet points out how Yahweh has sent famine, then drought, then blight, mildew, pestilence, and the like, but in each case the result is: "Yet you did not turn unto me!" Finally the prophet says, "Therefore, . . . prepare to meet your God, O Israel!" The purpose of natural disasters had been to lead Israel to repentance, but they had

---

[3] Theophile J. Meek, *Hebrew Origins* (New York: Harper, 1936), pp. 92-110.

failed; now Israel must be prepared to meet the punishment of God.

Later prophets proclaimed God's work in nature in the creation and sustaining of the cosmos. It may be that this emphasis appeared first in Second Isaiah. Passages in earlier prophets speaking of creation, such as Amos 4:13; 5:8; 9:5-6; Jer. 10:10-13, are probably late additions to those books. Second Isaiah did not believe, however, that Yahweh's work in creation was an absolutely finished thing; Yahweh was ever creating in history that which could be proclaimed as *new*.

The prophets show a deeper feeling of the close kinship existing between what we call the animate—including man—and the inanimate aspects of nature than is usually felt in modern times. Inanimate nature experiences the judgment of God, and also rejoices with man in his joy. Much of this is poetry, but it has a basis in a type of thought which does not distinguish so sharply as we do between man, the animals, and inanimate nature.

A few passages in the prophets will illustrate this. The very opening words of Amos' book, following a prose introduction, are:

> The Lord roars from Zion,
> And from Jerusalem utters his voice:
> The pastures of shepherds mourn,
> And the top of Carmel withers.

Isaiah, we have observed, announced that the Day of Yahweh was to be a time of judgment upon pride, not only in man, but also in nature; it would touch even the cedars of Lebanon, the oaks of Bashan, and all high mountains and lofty hills (Isa. 2:13-14).

A long passage in Jeremiah (5:22*b*-25) illustrates this feeling as well as a belief which is close to our concept of "natural law":

> I have set the sand as a bound for the sea,
> A perpetual barrier that it may not pass over;
> It may toss, but not prevail,
> Its waves may roar, but not pass over.

But this people has a straying and rebellious heart;
They have strayed continually.
They say not in their hearts:
"Let us fear the Lord our God,
Who gives the rain, both early and late,
In its season,
And keeps for us the weeks
Appointed for harvest."
Your iniquities have upset these things,
And your sins have withheld the good from you!

Second Isaiah poetically describes the rejoicing in nature which accompanies the joy of men over the redemption about to be wrought. This appears in the opening words of this poet-prophet:

The desert and dry land shall be glad,
The wilderness shall rejoice and blossom;
Like the crocus it shall blossom abundantly,
And be glad with joy and singing.
The glory of Lebanon shall be given it,
The splendor of Carmel and Sharon.
They shall behold the glory of the Lord,
The splendor of our God. (35:1-2.)

His work closes with a poem in similar mood, in which he says:

The mountains and hills shall break into singing before you,
And all the trees of the field shall clap their hands. (55:12*b*)

The close association which the prophets made between the world of inanimate nature and man's sins and joys leads us to summarize their view as being that nature, history, and man are one under the direct power of a personal God.

SOVEREIGN LORD
Another characteristic of the prophets' understanding of the nature of God has special importance for our consideration, in the next chapter, of sin and forgiveness.

As human beings the prophets had to use human analogies in their attempt to understand and teach the nature of deity. The analogies which they employed to express the relationship existing between God and man were most often analogies which have to do with the sovereignty and authority of God over men. God is Lord, King, Master, Ruler, and the like. The prophets—and other Old Testament writers—did sometimes employ the husband-wife or the father-son relationship, but not frequently. It may be that their infrequent use of such relationships was caused by a reaction to Canaanite religion, which was inclined to stress the physical features of those relationships, even when applied to deities.[4] Furthermore, we should not forget that the Hebrews believed the husband had great authority over the wife, and the father great power over the son— far more than American husbands and fathers are wont to claim or exercise. When Old Testament writers spoke of God as father or of Israelites as son, they implied his demand for obedience and loyal service as often as his care and solicitude.

In the light of our own social and political customs, and our interpretation of the New Testament teaching about the fatherhood of God, it is easy for us to misunderstand this prophetic emphasis on God's sovereignty and authority. We must remember that the Hebrews did not live in a political democracy; they did not elect presidents and legislative representatives. They lived in a monarchy. When they were politically independent, their monarchy was not as absolute as many ancient Oriental monarchies. They emphasized the responsibilities of their kings both to God and to the people under their rule. In practice some of their kings were benevolent and some were despotic. At any rate, it was natural for them to think of their God as King; even when they employed the nomadic figure of "shepherd" for human rulers or the divine ruler, they knew that shepherds have authority as well as loving solicitude.

The New Testament teaches very clearly that God is Father, but

---

[4] See G. E. Wright, "The Terminology of Old Testament Religion and Its Significance," *Journal of Near Eastern Studies*, I (1942), 404-14.

it is entirely erroneous for us to suppose that in this respect it differs from the Old. The difference is one of emphasis more than anything else; the New Testament lays stress on this teaching more than the Old, and it individualizes the fatherhood of God more than the Old Testament. But even in the Old Testament, Yahweh was the father of individuals as well as of the nation.[5] Furthermore, New Testament writers knew that a father has power and authority as well as love. We do an injustice to Christian teaching if we think of our God as a decrepit grandfather, as modern romanticists sometimes are inclined to do.

If God is King and Ruler over men, it follows that the primary duty of man is to obey and serve him. Man is the servant of God: he should be the loyal son. But he does not serve an arbitrary and irrational despot. One of the great contributions of the prophets was to establish firmly the belief that God himself is moral, and that his laws and judgments are not arbitrary. His anger is not irrational and childish, but an anger which springs from a morally responsible attitude toward his subjects and children.

[5] The passages which use the father-son relationship are conveniently listed and discussed by J. L. McKenzie, "The Divine Sonship of Men in the Old Testament," *The Catholic Biblical Quarterly*, VII (1945), 326-39.

CHAPTER X

THE PROPHETIC VIEW OF SIN AND FORGIVENESS

THE OLD TESTAMENT IS MORE OFTEN CONCERNED WITH SINS THAN WITH sin. Its writers have a great deal to say concerning attitudes and actions which are sinful; but they do not present a carefully reasoned theory of sin, its origin, and its nature. This is because of the nature of Hebrew thought, which was usually concrete rather than theoretical. Nevertheless, we may derive from the Old Testament a profound understanding of the nature of sin and of the forgiveness which is available to the sinner.

THE PROPHETIC THEORY OF SIN

The prophets believed that Yahweh was a God of mercy and love, but their emphasis was nearly always on the authority which God exerted upon man and the consequent demand he made for obedience and loyalty. We noted in the last chapter that the figures most frequently employed for the relationship between God and man are derived from fields in which authority is implied: ruler and subject, master and servant, husband and wife, and the like.

Since the prophets thus emphasized the authority of God and the duty of man to obey his sovereign will, they viewed sin as being primarily *rebellion* against God. This is well expressed in a Hebrew noun often used for sin, commonly translated in English by "transgression." The verb "transgress" (Hebrew *pāsha'*) is used in the Old Testament in a secular sense concerning Israel's revolt, under Jeroboam, against Rehoboam (I Kings 12:19); concerning Moab's rebellion against Israel (II Kings 1:1); and elsewhere. The use of such a word in a religious sense for the sin of man against God is entirely appropriate to the prophetic view. In its inner aspect sin is revolt against the authority of God, failure to recognize his sovereignty, disobedience to a higher will, because man places his own will or the sovereignty of someone else above the sovereign power of Almighty God. In its outer aspect, then, sin is a deviation from a moral standard set up by God. This is expressed in words for sin that mean literally "missing a mark," "erring from the right way," and the like. To the prophets, as we have observed, the standards of God have to do with morality, primarily with the relations of men to one another in society, and not with cultic sanctity and sacrifice.

This view of sin as rebellion is expressly stated by some of the prophets. For example, Isaiah says:

> Hear, O heavens, and give ear, O earth!
>   For the Lord has spoken:
> "I have nurtured and raised up sons,
>   But they rebelled against me.
> The ox knows his master,
>   And the ass his owner's crib,
> But Israel does not know,
>   My people has no understanding!" (1:2-3.)

Again, the same prophet says:

> Woe to rebellious[1] sons
>   (Says the Lord),
> Who take counsel, but not from me,
>   And make a league, but not by my spirit,
> To pile up sin upon sin. (30:1.)

Jeremiah describes Israel as a people that has "a straying and rebellious heart" (5:23). To Ezekiel, Israel was always "a rebellious house" (2:5, and often).

The rebellion of the Israelites against their God, to follow after deities which were really weak and unprofitable, appeared to the

---

[1] In this and the two following passages the verb used is not *pasha*ʿ, but a closely related Hebrew word. I do not imply that statistically the verb which meant literally "to rebel" was used more often than others. The idea of rebellion is, nevertheless, basic in the prophetic view of sin.

prophets to be an unnatural procedure contrary to common sense and reason. It seemed to be a demonstration of low intelligence, especially in view of the practice of other nations and of occurrences in nature. In Isa. 1:2-3, quoted immediately above, the prophet implies that men have not as much knowledge as an ox or an ass.

Jeremiah was greatly impressed with the unnaturalness of rebellion against God. In 2:10-11 he says:

> Pass over to the Grecian isles and see,
>   Send to Kedar and make careful inquiry,
>   See whether the like of this has ever occurred:
> Has a nation changed gods,
>   And they are no-gods?
> Yet my people have changed their glory [Yahweh]
>   For that which is useless!

In another passage (8:7) he contrasts Israel's actions with phenomena of the natural world:

> Even the stork in the heaven
>   Knows her seasons,
> The turtledove, swallow, and swift
>   Observe the time of their coming,
> But my people do not know
>   The ordinance of the Lord!

Again (18:13-15) Jeremiah says:

> Inquire among the nations:
>   Who has heard the like of this?
> The virgin Israel
>   Has done a very horrible thing!
> Does the snow of Lebanon vanish
>   From the crest of Sirion?
> Do its trickling waters dry up,
>   Its cold, flowing streams?
> Yet my people have forgotten me,
>   And burned incense to empty idols!

This unnatural and senseless rebellion against their God could come, the prophets thought, only from corruption in men's hearts. It is characteristic of the prophets that they did not stop with giving moral advice, but went on to describe the inner nature of sin and to find its roots in the evil of the human heart. "Moral counsel belongs to the task of true prophecy," says Reinhold Niebuhr. "But if this moral counsel is not informed by a profound understanding of the human heart it will be easily tempted to regard some partial victory over human sin as the ultimate victory. It will fail to see how perennially and inevitably the human soul is involved in the self-defeat of sin, no matter what level of righteousness it achieves."[2]

Among the Old Testament prophets, it is Jeremiah who stresses more than others the role of the heart in the origin of sin. Frequently he refers sin to the "stubbornness of the evil heart" (7:24; 9:14; 13:10, et al.). He says of the heart:

> The heart is more deceitful than all things, and very sick—
>   Who can know it?
> I the Lord am a searcher of the heart
>   And tester of the conscience,
> Giving to every man according to his ways,
>   According to the fruit of his doings. (17:9-10.)

Concerning Judah's sin he declares:

> The sin of Judah is written
>   With an iron pen,
> Engraved with the point of a diamond
>   On the tablet of their heart. (17:1.)

It is no wonder that Jeremiah emphasizes strongly the need of repentance, and that the "new covenant" is one in which the law is to be written on the hearts of men. We should remember that in Hebrew psychology the heart was considered the seat of the intelli-

[2] *Beyond Tragedy* (New York: Scribner, 1937), pp. 106-7.

gence, not simply of the emotions. Often it would be entirely accurate to translate the Hebrew word as "mind" rather than "heart."

Jesus' view regarding the nature and origin of sin was similar to that of the Old Testament prophets. His teachings have little to say in a theoretical or abstract way regarding sin. He talked of sins and he associated with sinners much more intimately than did religious leaders of his time. But to him, as to the older prophets, sin was rebellion against the authority of God. He spoke more often of God as father than as ruler, but there can be no doubt that the fatherhood of God in Jesus' teaching included God's sovereignty. In the Kingdom of God it is God the Father who is or will be king, and God the Father demands of his children loyal obedience.

The prophetic teaching regarding the importance of a pure heart was fundamental to the teaching of Jesus. In the Beatitudes it is "the pure in heart" who "see God" (Matt. 5:8). In the long passage in the Sermon on the Mount in which Jesus reinterprets the old laws regarding murder and adultery (Matt. 5:21-32), he stresses the supreme importance of the intention or desire existing within one's mind. Jesus could not care for the meticulous ceremonial rules of the Pharisees, for he realized that evils come from the heart, not from that which enters the stomach (Mark 7:1-23).

It is often observed that the prophets considered sin to be largely social in its nature—that is, that it consisted of man's mistreatment of his neighbor in a great variety of ways. This is largely true, but it is an error to suppose that the prophets thought of man as sinning against man. When he did wrong to his neighbor, the prophets believed, man sinned against God. It was just because they had such a lofty view of God and the importance of obeying his will that they considered man's sin of oppressing or otherwise maltreating his neighbor to be so serious. The author of the fifty-first psalm said:

> Against thee, thee only, have I sinned,
> And done evil in thy sight!

The prodigal son finally decided to go to his father and confess his sin by saying, "Father I have sinned against heaven [that is, God], and in thy sight" (Luke 15:18). Both passages express the view that sin, although it may primarily affect one's social relationships, is a sin against God. The prophets believed that God is grieved by wrongdoing toward one's neighbor precisely because he valued the lives of all men and because wrong social relations were a denial of his demand that men be "the people of God."

THE PROPHETIC DEMAND FOR REPENTANCE

The prophets believed that all men are sinners because of the corruptness of their hearts. Men have rebelled against God and thus alienated themselves from him. Do the Old Testament prophets have anything to say regarding deliverance from sin? Most assuredly they do, and their answer is closely akin to the familiar New Testament answer, although it is not expressed in the same way. They say that men must repent of their sin and seek the forgiveness of God.

If one studies the Old Testament with a concordance to the English Bible, he may conclude that it has little to say regarding repentance and forgiveness. A cursory glance will show that in the English Bible the words "repent," "repentance," "forgive," and "forgiveness" occur rarely in the Old Testament in comparison with their frequency in the New Testament. This is because Old Testament writers express the ideas of repentance and forgiveness with other words and sometimes by circumlocutions.

The proper word for "repent," *nāham,* is used in the Old Testament more often for God's change of mind or purpose than for man's. Sometimes when used of men it has a secular sense, with little religious connotation. Actually, the idea of repentance in the Old Testament is most often expressed by a Hebrew word, *shūb,* which literally means "to turn" or "to return." This word has two directly opposite meanings, and we can determine only from the context which meaning is intended in a specific passage. Sometimes it means to turn away from God, and a noun derived from the verb may mean "backsliding" or "apostasy." But the same verb may mean to turn *to* God in repentance and to seek from him healing and forgiveness. Both meanings occur in a single sentence in Jer. 8:4:

> If men fall will they not rise?
> If one turns away, will he not return?

In this verse, turning away from God is equivalent to falling, but returning to him is equivalent to rising and coming back toward God.

In the King James Version this word *shūb* is translated "repent" in three passages: I Kings 8:47; Ezek. 14:6; 18:30. We should do entire justice to Old Testament religion by frequently translating it thus.

The prophetic understanding of the nature of repentance is expressed especially well in two passages in Hosea and one in Jeremiah. The first is Hos. 5:15–6:2. The prophet represents God as determining to forsake the people as the result of their sin—especially idolatry—until they shall seek him in repentance.

> I will return again to my place,
>   Until they acknowledge their guilt
> And seek my presence:
>   In their affliction they will seek me [saying]:
> "Come, let us return unto the Lord,
>   For he has torn, but will heal us;
> He has smitten, but will bind us up;
>   He will revive us after two days;
> On the third day will raise us up
>   That we may live in his presence."

The other passage in Hosea is 14:1-3, which is similar both in idea and in form:

> Return, O Israel, unto the Lord your God,
>   For you have stumbled in your iniquity.
> Take with you words,

> And return unto the Lord;
> Say to him, all of you:
> "Take away iniquity,
> And we will take what is good,
> And requite thee with the fruit of our lips.
> Assyria will not save us,
> Nor will we ride on horses.
> We will say no more, 'Our gods!'
> To the work of our own hands."

Jeremiah was greatly influenced by Hosea, and early in his career he summoned the people to repent and seek God's forgiveness. This message is well expressed in Jer. 3:12-13:

> Repent, O apostate Israel (says the Lord).
> I will not frown upon you,
> For I am faithful (says the Lord),
> And will not be angry forever.
> Only acknowledge your iniquity,
> That you have rebelled against the Lord your God,
> And scattered your favors among strangers under every
> green tree,
> And have not hearkened to my voice.

In addition to these there are many other passages in which prophets summoned their hearers to repent, with the promise that God would forgive if they turned to him. A familiar passage in Isaiah (30:15) may accurately be rendered:

> By repentance and resting [on God] shall you be saved;
> In quietness and in confidence shall be your strength.

For the Old Testament prophets, returning to God, or repentance, involved both one's mind or heart and one's actions. It meant a change of mind and purpose in which one renounced his rebellion and determined to obey God's will and hearken to his voice, and this had its natural consequence in a change of action in which justice and righteousness supplanted injustice and unrighteousness. The prophets always believed that men must, in the words of John the Baptist, "bring forth fruit worthy of repentance" (Matt. 3:8). For Amos, seeking good or loving the good involved, among other things, establishing justice in the gate (5:15). Isaiah called upon his hearers to cease doing evil and to learn to do that which was good —to seek justice, to restrain the robber, and to help the fatherless and widow (1:17). Similar passages might be cited from all the prophets. They would hardly have recognized as genuine repentance any change of attitude which did not lead to changed actions.

Jesus of Nazareth fits clearly the pattern of the prophet in his summons to men to repent. According to Mark, his first words uttered after the beginning of his public ministry included "Repent ye." That summons to repentance ran through his entire career. Jesus did not call upon men to be good; he did not ask them to aid in building or in bringing in the Kingdom of God. He summoned them to repent in order that they might be prepared to enter or to receive the Kingdom of God. But also, like the Old Testament prophets, he knew that true repentance would lead men to bring forth fruit worthy of their profession. In the Sermon on the Mount he reminded his hearers that men could be known by their fruits. "Not everyone who says to me, 'Lord, Lord,' shall enter into the Kingdom of heaven, but he who does the will of my Father in heaven." (Matt. 7:21.) The test to be applied to men in the great judgment was whether they had fed the hungry, given drink to the thirsty, taken in strangers, clothed the naked, and visited the sick and imprisoned (Matt. 25:31-46).

The prophets of the Old Testament held in view the nation as a whole more than Jesus did. Yet all effective repentance must be individual. The book of Jonah presents a picture in which all of Nineveh, people and king, men and beasts, repented at the preaching of Jonah. But the book of Jonah is parable rather than history, and such wholesale repentance has never been known to occur. The best that the prophets hoped for was the repentance of a remnant, composed of individuals, who should turn to God and be preserved through the day of calamity predicted by the prophets.

GOD'S READINESS TO FORGIVE

A summons to repentance from sin implies that God will forgive those who do repent. Let us consider in more detail the prophets' belief that their God was ready to forgive.

The words "forgive" and "forgiveness" rarely appear in the English Old Testament. The Hebrew language most often expresses the concept of forgiveness by metaphors, such as "take away sin," "pass over sin," "cover up sin," "blot out sin," "remember not sin," and "heal." These are of frequent occurrence, and the belief that Yahweh was a God of forgiveness was present from early times in Israel.[3] Furthermore, in the minds of the prophets the idea of forgiveness was closely related to, and sometimes implied in, the ideas of redemption or salvation.

The proper Hebrew word for "forgive" is *sālah.* One of its earliest appearances in the Old Testament was in the prayer of Amos 7:2. The prophet prayed that God would forgive Israel and refrain from destroying her by a locust plague. On this occasion the prophet's prayer was heard; Yahweh "repented," changing his purpose toward the nation. The naturalness of this prayer suggests that the belief in Yahweh's forgiving nature was much older than Amos, and such a belief is evidenced in earlier literature. For example, Exod. 34:6-7 describes Yahweh as "a God merciful and gracious, slow to anger and abundant in faithfulness and truth, showing his faithfulness to thousands, forgiving [literally, taking away] iniquity and transgression and sin."

This quotation reveals the fundamental ground for God's forgiveness as the prophets conceived it: it was primarily because of God's own nature that God forgave man when he repented. They

---

[3] An extensive recent study of the Old Testament doctrines of redemption and forgiveness is J. J. Stamm, *Erlösen und Vergeben im Alten Testament* (Bern: A. Francke, 1940).

best expressed the idea in the phrase "for my name's sake" and closely related expressions, used especially by Ezekiel—who may have originated it—and Second Isaiah. Ezekiel taught that the only reason Yahweh had not destroyed Israel much sooner in her rebellion was for his own name's sake (20:9, 14, 22), and for the same reason he would restore the nation in the future (36:22). As used by Ezekiel the idea contained the notion of Yahweh's jealousy for his honor, but in Hebrew usage "name" stood for one's whole personality or character. The phrase therefore suggested that it was because of his fundamentally merciful nature that God forgave. Second Isaiah used similar terms, as in 43:25:

> I—even I—am he who blots out your iniquity for my own sake,
> And your sin I shall no longer remember.

The prophets were not alone among Old Testament writers in believing that Yahweh was a forgiving God. All Hebrews believed this. The priests believed that God forgave men, not that they could themselves forgive. Many of the psalms contain prayers for forgiveness. The unique characteristic of the prophets, as distinguished from the priests, is that they thought forgiveness was available to men without the accompaniment of sacrifice. Man must only acknowledge his guilt and turn to God, seeking his grace. We have already considered the prophetic attitude toward the sacrificial system; since the majority of the prophets opposed that system, they could not have thought it essential that men should bring sacrifices to God in order to obtain forgiveness. We may also note the example of Isaiah: in his temple vision he believed that the seraph pronounced his sin forgiven without sacrifice being offered (6:7).

Forgiveness of sin, in the teaching of the prophets, did not necessarily imply that men would escape from punishment, nor even that they would receive moderation of their punishment. Sometimes, of course, forgiveness meant escape from an intended punishment, as in the case of Amos' prayer in 7:2.[4] But sometimes forgiveness

---

[4] Discussed above, pp. 38-39.

would come only after full punishment. This is best shown in the words of Second Isaiah, who constantly proclaims God's forgiveness and redemption of Israel. Yet his work is based upon the belief that Israel has already—apparently through the Babylonian exile—received from the Lord's hand double for all her sins. Still the Lord can say in the verse in which forgiveness and redemption are most closely associated in the Old Testament:

> I have blotted out as a dark cloud your transgressions,
>> And as a mist your sins;
> Return unto me, for I have redeemed you! (44:22.)

To the prophets, the essential element in forgiveness is not the escape or mitigation of punishment for sin but the restoration of man to the status of obedience to God and fellowship with him—a condition which he was created to fulfill and enjoy. Forgiveness means that the barrier between man and God created by sin is removed, and man receives new impetus and strength for a life of justice, righteousness, and truth.

CHAPTER XI

PROPHETIC RELIGION

HAVING CONSIDERED IN DETAIL THE PROPHETS AND THEIR DISTINCTIVE viewpoints on various topics, let us undertake to summarize the most significant elements of prophetic religion as we have seen it exhibited in the work and lives of the great Old Testament prophets and Jesus.

1. Prophetic religion insists that religious leadership, which involves speaking for God to men and for men to God, is a sacred trust to be discharged with the utmost sincerity and devotion. All religious leaders and authorities must have a deep sense of vocation, of being called and commissioned by God to perform a mission and preach a message in his name. Prophetic religion opposes all flippancy, insincerity, and hypocrisy, and condemns every kind of exploitation.

The religious leader must be one who both speaks and lives for God. The true prophet was always a man of unimpeachable character, attempting to live according to his ideals. The Old Testament prophet was not sinless, and himself stood in need of God's forgiveness, but his will was directed toward the doing of God's will in his personal life as well as in his preaching. The false prophet was denounced for his low moral character as well as for his attitude of false optimism.

Prophetic religion does not consider popular ideals of success as adequate for the man who would speak for God. God's spokesman must be prepared to accept unpopularity and failure—in the usual sense—as his immediate reward. Fidelity to his God must be his chief aim.

2. Prophetic religion insists that *all* of the life of *all* men comes under the judgment of God, and therefore of his prophetic representative. Life must not be compartmentalized. Religion must not

174

be relegated to a corner of life or personality or time. It must be at the very core of life itself. Furthermore, no class in society is exempt from the prophet's criticism.

The prophets condemned such things as pride, narrowness in vision, and abuse of power, of all kinds, because these sins involved attempts to compartmentalize life and to leave God's will out of certain of its phases. For the individual and for the nation the word "all" is of fundamental importance: *all* of an individual's life must be submitted to God's will, and *all* members of the nation must be considered as equal members of the people of God. Essential democracy owes much to the prophets' insistence on human brotherhood and equality before God.

3. Prophetic religion has much to teach us regarding the interpretation of history. It insists that all of history is under the control of the God of power and love. The past must not be sharply separated from the future, and one must not make the error of believing that God has manifested himself only in events of the past. Time is real. This present world is real and significant. God has a purpose in time, and history is an unfolding of that purpose. History is moving to a goal and a consummation. The same God who has been worthy of trust in the past is worthy also of trust for the future. This is the basic hope of both prophets and apocalyptists regarding the future; this is the abiding truth amid numerous details which have for us only temporary significance.

4. Prophetic religion insists that the demands of God are always moral demands. The God of justice and mercy and truth must be served and worshiped by the doing of justice and mercy and truth. The prophets were not *mere* moralists, but they believed that morality was of basic and indispensable importance to religion. They would not have said that all beliefs and actions must be judged by their moral effectiveness, but they could never have thought that any immoral belief or action could be true. To some of the prophets all formal ritual appeared an offense to God. The ultimate prophetic viewpoint is that formal ritual must always serve to inspire and inform righteous living.

5. Prophetic ideals of patriotism insist that a nation must be courageous enough to criticize its own actions and policies, and not exhaust its energy simply in hating the enemy. Accordingly, the true patriot must seek the total welfare of all the people of his own land, but not at the expense of those in other lands. Prophetic religion opposes exploitation of the masses by their leaders, and division into proud national groupings. It teaches that patriotism which looks only to immediate national advantage is shortsighted and false. A wide view of mankind based upon a profound understanding of the sphere of God's sovereignty will inform all true love of country.

6. While the prophets were always interested in proclaiming truer ideas of God, they were more concerned to call men to deeper experiences of the living God and to summon them to submit themselves more unreservedly to his authority. They taught that God is sufficient for all the various needs of men. Half-gods and false idols must go, so that the true and living God may rule. The only way of salvation for men and nations is the way of obedience to the God of justice and mercy, of nature and history.

7. The prophets believed that sin is rebellion against a sovereign God and rises from corruption of the heart. Their view of sin was serious because their view of God's nature was serious. To them, sin often involves maltreatment of one's neighbor and wrong social relations, but it is basically an offense against God and a flaunting of his authority.

The prophets believed that man can be delivered from sin by repentance. God is ever willing to forgive the penitent "for his own name's sake." They believed that forgiveness was available without sacrifice to God—other than the sacrifice of a humble and contrite heart. Forgiveness does not necessarily bring removal or moderation of punishment, but it removes the barrier erected between man and God by man's rebellion.

8. Prophetic religion deals in principles. It does not set up blueprints for the ideal society, nor does it profess to see in detail into

the remote future. The Old Testament prophets dealt with specific problems in their own times in terms of their understanding of eternal principles. Some of their solutions to temporary problems have only historical interest for us today. But every age has the obligation to apply prophetic principles to the solution of its own problems, using for the task its every resource of devotion, research, imagination and insight.

INDEX OF SCRIPTURE REFERENCES

179

INDEX OF NAMES AND SUBJECTS